THE JUNK FOOD VEGETARIAN

JONATHAN CAINER

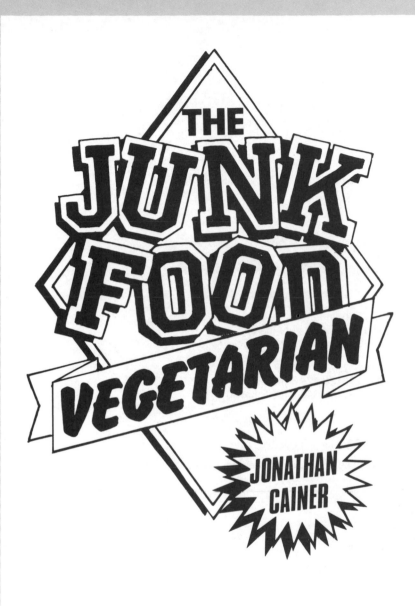

THE JUNK FOOD VEGETARIAN

JONATHAN CAINER

PIATKUS

THE JUNK FOOD VEGETARIAN
Jonathan Cainer

© 1985 Jonathan Cainer
First published in 1985
by Judy Piatkus (Publishers) Limited, London

British Library Cataloguing in Publication Data

Cainer, Jonathan
  The Junk Food Vegetarian
  1. Vegetarian cookery
  1. Title
  641.5′636   TX837
ISBN 0 86188 479 5 (hardback)
     0 86188 343 8 (paperback)

Designed by Ken Leeder

Typeset by Phoenix Photosetting, Chatham
Printed at The Bath Press, Avon

CONTENTS

(the LAST thing you need to know!)

1
INTRODUCTION

WHAT'S A JUNK FOOD VEGETARIAN?

Vegetarians are people who, for moral, spiritual or dietary reasons, choose not to eat meat, and for the purpose of this book meat includes fish and eggs.* In a society where dead flesh is the normal thing to eat, this tends to put us on the defensive.

My parents are Vegetarians. As a child, I remember my grandmother trying to 'sneak some meat down me'. She believed it was her duty.

As I grew up, Californian film stars and Liverpudlian pop singers made Vegetarianism more fashionable. By the early Seventies it was the 'hip thing to do'. It was also hip to eat wholefoods.

Wholefoods are things like brown rice and adzuki beans. They taste terrible but they're terribly good for you. Most Vegetarians eat a lot of wholefoods. Deep down inside, they worry about not eating meat. What if they're depriving themselves? To assuage this guilt, they indulge in an orgy of masochism, munching mountains of muesli, millet and mung beans. It's the sackcloth and ashes syndrome.

JUNK FOOD VEGETARIANS DON'T PLAY THAT GAME.

The wholefood fanatics have had it their own way too long. If you want to spend your life boiling beans, riding bicycles and getting 'back to the earth' you can join them.

This book is dedicated to everyone who likes canned soup, frozen pizzas, processed peas, packet curries and instant whip. If your desire to be Vegetarian is NOT tied up with a fear of technology, a love of washing up or a fetish for beansprouts . . . welcome aboard!

---

* Whether or not a true Vegetarian could or should eat eggs is very much a personal matter. If you do want to include eggs in your diet, you will find hundreds of books on the market that deal with how to cook them. Some of them even have the word VEGETARIAN in their titles.

2

NUTRITION

DEBUNKING THE WHOLEFOOD MYTH

Before writing this chapter I read 19 recent and weighty tomes on nutrition. This is what I learned:

1. Human beings need food.

2. Food contains things like minerals, vitamins, protein, dietary fibre, carbohydrates and calories. Some foods contain more of these things than others. No one food contains them all.

3. If we eat far too much of any of the above, we get sick.

4. If we eat far too little of any of the above, we get sick.

5. No one really knows how much is far too much and how little is far too little.* Although no one really knows, some people have some pretty strong opinions: High Fibre; Low Protein; High Protein; Low Fibre; Low Sugar; Extra Minerals; Low Calories; High Carbohydrates; Low Sodium; Low Animal Fat; Extra Vitamins; No Extra Vitamins; No Gluten; High Polyunsaturates; etc.
These diets come in and out of style faster than some pop stars.

---

* Most governments publish a list of 'recommended minimum daily intakes for the average person'. There is, of course, no such thing as an 'average person'. Even if there was, nutritionists disagree quite heatedly about what she or he requires. It's a difficult thing to research because even when you can get human volunteers, you can't keep them in a laboratory all their lives. New information keeps changing things, and the minimum protein requirement, for example, goes up and down like a yo-yo.
On the whole, however, it's easier to pick out minimums (how much Vitamin C do you need to cure scurvy?) than maximums. The reason why maximums are hard to establish is worth reading about. It's also the reason why you should take 'food scares' with a pinch of salt (or salt substitute!).
First of all, you have to find out how much of something it takes to kill a laboratory rat. This means starting with a fatal dose and then working slowly backwards until you find the highest amount it can eat without getting sick. The maximum amount

Mainly, you find them in books with exciting titles like **The Shocking Facts about . . .**

In general, the more scientific people don't have such strong opinions. They seem to agree that as long as you eat a little of lots of different things, you shouldn't come to any harm.

Unless you suffer from a particular deficiency or allergy, they're probably right. Sadly, this advice normally comes in books with boring titles such as, **Recent Advances in Therapeutic Nutrition**.

A real Junk Food Vegetarian wouldn't bother with this chapter. They'd take a multi vitamin pill with minerals once a day and wash it down with a protein supplement. Then, they could eat what the heck they liked!!!

A SELECTION OF POPULAR MYTHS AND LEGENDS . . .

1 *VEGETARIANS DON'T GET ENOUGH PROTEIN* (or they aren't getting the right sort of protein).

Unless you are a *Vegan* (no milk or cheese) this is *not true*. Short of living on sugar and cooking fat, you can't help but get sufficient balanced protein in the food you eat.

2 *THERE ARE SOME VITAMINS THAT A VEGETARIAN DOESN'T GET.*

Once again, only Vegans need worry. Vitamin B12 is the item in question and there's plenty in milk and cheese. (Incidentally, you can store Vitamin B12 in your body for up to 5 years.)

---

then considered safe for a human is usually *one hundredth* of the most a *rat* can take each day of its life.

Scientists have reputations to keep, so they always err on the safe side, i.e. when something like 'saccharin' is declared a possible carcinogen, it does not mean that it has ever caused cancer in a human, simply that, when fed in incredibly large doses to laboratory animals over a long period of time, some of them got cancer.

It is the same thing for sugar and coronary thrombosis, animal fats and serum cholesterol, sodium and blood pressure, etc. Scientists have not conclusively proved any of these links. They have merely raised suspicions. These suspicions are themselves under suspicion by other scientists!

It helps to remember that:

1. Anything, even water, is fatal when administered in high enough doses.

2. Artificial additives (preservatives, colours, flavours and emulsifiers) are the most closely watched of all ingredients, and therefore probably the safest.

3 SUGAR IS BAD FOR YOU.

Sugar appears to have no nutritional value but it's only *too much sugar* that can be bad for you. How much is too much? No one really knows, but your dentist might have some strong opinions!

4 TOO MUCH SALT IS BAD FOR YOU.

. . . according to the latest scientific evidence, this is largely a myth. Even those who are allergic to salt will find that the salt they put in processed food is not the problem! – it's the way we automatically drown our dinner in the stuff, before we even taste it, that is bad for us!

5 ONLY FRESH, RAW FOOD IS GOOD FOR YOU.

Nature, in her wisdom, supplies fruit and veg with an abundance of goodness. Yes, it starts losing vitamins as soon as it's picked. Yes, it loses more in the chopping and yes . . . even more in the cooking, *but* (unless you stew it silly) there's still plenty left for the eating! The frozen, canned or dried variety can be even more nourishing than the stuff you buy from the greengrocers because it's treated quicker.

(Carnivores may be interested to know that raw fish and raw eggs contain antivitamins. These delightful organisms actually *destroy* certain vitamins in your body. So much for Sushi!)

6 YOU NEED VITAMIN C EVERY DAY.

Of all the vitamins, it seems Vitamin C is the most easily offended. You only have to look at it and it storms off in a huff! One of the places you can sneak up on it is in orange juice (even the stuff made from concentrate has plenty), and it also likes French fried potatoes. Once you catch some, it takes up to 30 days to escape, though I shouldn't wait quite that long to restock!

7 WHITE BREAD IS BAD FOR YOU.

Both brown and white bread are high in protein, B vitamins and minerals. Besides the fact that brown bread can taste like sawdust, the only major nutritional difference is *dietary fibre*.

Dietary Fibre is what Grandma used to call 'roughage', and bakers call bran. It helps keep you 'regular'. Now read on very carefully . . .

White bread has the bran taken out of it to make it taste nicer.

Meat contains *no* dietary fibre. It takes much longer to digest and it gets 'clogged' in the body. So *meat eaters need the extra roughage in wholemeal bread.*

BUT . . .

Almost *every vegetable* is packed with dietary fibre. Vegetarians can't avoid it, even if they try! Therefore, *Vegetarians don't need extra roughage.*

The vitamins in white flour are just as good for you as those in brown, though they may come from a synthetic source. Ironically enough, this seems to offend the very people who happily swallow synthesized vitamin pills.

8 BROWN RICE IS BETTER FOR YOU THAN WHITE RICE.

Brown rice tastes like stewed boots because of all the dietary fibre in it. Once again, Vegetarians don't really need to inflict this torture on themselves.

White rice in Britain does not have added vitamins (though it does in the USA). It is still good for protein and as long as your diet is varied, you won't be missing much if it is not enriched. (If you've really got a heavy white rice habit, you'll find parboiled or converted rice [like Uncle B**s] offers a better deal on the vitamin front.)

9 CHEMICALS ARE BAD FOR YOU.

What would you rather eat, a fresh tomato or the following . . .? Methyl Salicylate, Phenylethanol, Ethylphenol, Caprilic acid, Trans-6-methyl-3, 5-Heptadiene2-one, 5,6-Epoxyionone, Geranylacetone, 0-Hydroxyacetophenome, Benzaldehyde, Propionic acid, Heptadienal . . .?

Sorry to be 'clever clever' but these are just a few of the ingredients in the 'aroma' of a fresh tomato. We haven't even started on the fruit itself.

It's interesting how sodium chloride and acetic acid sounds so much more terrifying than salt and vinegar!

10 PROCESSED FOODS ARE 'UNNATURAL'.

Is a symphony more or less natural than the song of the birds? The earliest food technologists were cavemen. Raw berries were boring and bitter. They dried them, pounded them, mixed the resulting powder with water and cooked it over hot stones. It wasn't quite Wonderloaf but the principle remains the same!

It may not be strictly 'necessary' to make food more palatable by cooking, spicing or shaping it but it has certainly always been popular. Some people might even call it creative. Today, we can not only synthesize all known nutrients, but also taste, texture and colour. Food technology means that, in principle, no one in the world need ever starve again. It is now only the politicians who are standing in the way.

11 FOOD ADDITIVES ARE HARMLESS. CAN WE BE SURE?

Even the purest of organically grown vegetables contain natural poisons. Who knows what the accumulative effect of all that 'natural' arsenic, cyanide and oxalic acid in our food could be. In fact, it is now possible to synthesize all the goodness in a certain food and leave out the poisons that occur in the real thing.

All I'm saying, is that not everything in nature is wonderful just as not everything that comes out of a laboratory is evil. Isn't it a bit ironic that the very scientists whose words are taken as gospel when they declare that 'Animal fats may lead to heart disease' are the same people who are bitterly mistrusted when they say: 'Sodium Benzoate is a perfectly safe preservative.'

12 FACTORY FOOD GIVES YOU BAD KARMA.

No comment.

13 TEA AND COFFEE ARE DANGEROUS.

Not as dangerous as crossing the road, smoking, mountaineering, having an affair with someone else's spouse, or living under the constant threat of global thermonuclear war! (Fresh coffee, by the way, contains a B vitamin, niacin. The stronger you drink it, the more you get!)

3
WASHING UP AND HOW TO AVOID IT

There may be some people who *enjoy* washing up. I'm even told there are people who *enjoy* waiting for buses.

There are several ways to avoid this painful process.

METHOD 1

1. Stack all your dirty pans and dishes in a quiet corner. (The more you have, the longer you can go without facing the detergent.)

2. Invite some friends round on a Sunday afternoon. Casually offer to cook them dinner, and then say, *Oh gosh, I appear to have no clean pans left*.

3. With any luck, someone will volunteer to do your dirty work for you.

METHOD 2

Get smart . . .

1. Invest in some aluminium foil containers from your local freezer shop. Use them as baking or casserole dishes. Throw them away when you've finished. (Also you can get really good paper plates these days!)

2. Cook cans by immersing them, unopened, in a pan of boiling water. Contrary to popular opinion, they won't explode. Five minutes will cook the contents of anything except steamed pudding (see Chapter 8).

3. Frozen vegetables can be 'boiled in the bag' – the only problem is that you've got to eat the whole bagful. Just sling the bag in boiling water for 5 minutes. They'll always be just right!

4. Use non-stick pans.

5. Try not to burn things!!!

A GUIDED TOUR OF YOUR KITCHEN

KITCHEN UTENSILS

To cook any of the recipes in this book, the most you'll ever need is:

2 saucepans	1 *sharp* knife
1 large deep frying pan	2 casserole dishes
3 matching lids	1 flat baking tray
plastic spatula	1 measuring jug
1 wooden spoon	1 mixing bowl
1 serving spoon	1 cheese slicer
	a grater

Oh yes, and a CAN OPENER

If you're short on any of these, you can always use *ingenuity*. (Available from most department stores!)

FANCY STUFF

Do you own at least one of the following?

A deep freeze
A blender
A toasted sandwich maker
A microwave oven
A wok

If not, you'll be happy to hear that you *don't* need them to cook anything in this book. If you do, you'll already know how wonderful they are. With a little bit of ingenuity any of these recipes can be modified to accommodate your favourite toy.

DEPARTMENT OF WEIGHTS AND MEASURES

As you will hopefully have noticed by now, this is not really a conventional cookery book. None of the quantities given are crucial. The idea is definitely *not* to spend ages weighing things. I originally wanted to give recipes that called for a small can of this and a large packet of that plus a handful of those, then shake it around on your stove till it bubbles.

The following table is designed to help you adopt a looser style of cooking! (All conversions are VERY approximate!)

Solids . . .

Oz	Grams	Handfuls
½ oz	= 10g	= a big pinch
1 oz	= 25g	= a small handful
4 oz	= 110g	= quite a bit
8 oz	= 225g	= lots
1 lb	= 450g	= tons

Liquids . . .

1 teaspoon	= 5ml	= a few drops
1 tablespoon	= 15ml	= a puddle
5 fl oz	= 150ml	= dainty cup
10 fl oz	= 300ml	= a mugful
20 fl oz	= 570ml	= 2 big mugs
1¾ pints	= 1 litre	= gallons!

TEMPERATURES

Cordon Bleu this ain't! For the purposes of this book, there are only three settings on your cooker – low, medium and ouch! To find these equivalents on your oven, use this table . . .

GAS	ELECT		JFV
3	325°F	160°C	warm
5	375°F	190°C	medium
8	450°F	230°C	phew!

The higher the shelf, the quicker it cooks!

4
IF YOU'RE NEW TO COOKING

People new to cooking will find this section useful. If you're experienced, feel free to skip it. I don't want to teach my grandmother to suck egg replacer!

GOLDEN RULES AND BRASS TACKS . . .

It's easy. The object of the exercise is to apply heat to food till it tastes the way you like it.

● As a general rule, vegetables are nicer *undercooked* than *overcooked*.

● Canned food is already cooked and only needs *heating*. Warm it up gently on a low heat, stirring when necessary. If you're adding canned things to a stew, put them in *last*.

● Frozen food is surprisingly quick to cook, 'cos it was blanched (softened with steam) before it was frozen. Use less water than they say on the packet, and if you're adding it to a sauce or stew, just sling it straight in without water. You can also stir fry almost any frozen or fresh vegetable.

● *Herbs and spices* . . . There's no reason why a Junk Food Vegetarian shouldn't have an enormous spice cupboard. It takes no extra cooking time or effort to sling some oregano in your baked beans or cumin in your mushroom soup. The difference, however, can be phenomenal. A little gentle experimentation is all that's required. Go for fresh rather than dried (if you can), and use a little at a time till you get the flavour you fancy.

● *The trick with ALL cooking* . . . is to keep having a little taste. It's much easier than timing things. Everything but rice should be given the occasional shake or stir.

16

- *It is cooked when it tastes cooked*. The two most common mistakes are over or under cooking. Just 'cos it's bubbling at the edges, it doesn't mean it's warm in the middle. And yet, with the possible exception of beans, nothing improves with merciless stewing! You're the one who's going to eat it, so learn to trust your judgment rather than boringly timing everything.

- *The thicker the liquid the more stirring it needs*.

- *Keep it warm*. Suppose you're cooking two things at once and one is ready before the other. Put it in the oven on the lowest setting. If it's not in an oven-proof container, leave the oven door ajar and keep an eye on it.

- *If you really foul up* . . . chuck it out and start again! Don't force yourself to eat mistakes. Resist the temptation to mail your burnt potatoes to the starving millions. A fiver to Oxfam is more useful and it won't go bad in the post!

- *Don't panic!* You can always give up and go down the chip shop!

RIGHT! Let's start with something easy.

FILLERS

Most of the main-dish recipes in this book can be served with rice, potatoes or pasta. If you're new to cooking, here's how to make these starchy delights. (If you're on a diet, go easy on them. Use the salads in Chapter 6 instead, or you could just have double helpings of the main dish.)

ROAST POTATOES

They aren't quick, but they are easy. For 4 greedy people, you need 2 lbs of pre-washed big potatoes. Put the oven on quite hot.

You'll find that some potatoes are bigger than others. Give them a quick rinse and chop the big ones in half. (Leave the little ones as they are.) Get a roasting tray and pour 2 tablespoons of oil on to it. Swill it around and plonk on the potatoes. Shove 'em into the oven on the top shelf and forget about them for 40 minutes.

It's very hard to overcook roast potatoes. The longer you leave 'em, the crispier they get!

BAKED POTATOES

Buy large, pre-washed potatoes and whack the oven up high. Before putting them on the top shelf, pierce them with a fork. This will make them less likely to explode. Go away and listen to Beethoven's Ninth.

A WORD ABOUT CHIPS

Frozen oven chips have instructions on the packet.

Real chips, strictly speaking, involve too much effort for Junk Food Vegetarians. There are, however, some things in life worth making an effort for! Buy a bag of frozen chips or slice up some pre-washed potatoes (peeling is for sissies!). See the section on deep frying.

If all this sounds like too much effort, you could move next door to a chip shop.

BOILED POTATOES

. . . come in cans and taste delicious.

MASHED POTATOES

Heat your canned boiled potatoes, drain off most of the water and add copious quantities of butter. Pound mercilessly with a blunt instrument.

● Instant Mash improves tremendously if you use half milk, half water and add plenty of butter, chopped herbs or cheese.

(You need never, ever, ever, EVER peel potatoes!)

RICE

QUICKEST WAY . . .

Buy a can of precooked rice. Follow the instructions on it. Takes about 4 minutes!

EASIEST WAY . . .

Buy some 'boil-in-the-bag' rice. Shove it in a pan of boiling water for 15 minutes. Hey presto, no washing up!

HIGHFALUTIN WAY . . .

1 cup of rice to 2 cups of boiling water. (Yes, CUPS! Like what you drink tea out of!)

Put on a low heat, cover and leave for 10 minutes.

Don't stir! Serves 1–2 depending on size of cup.

PASTA

If you're lucky enough to live near a source of fresh pasta, ask the people in the shop how to cook it. Normally, 2 minutes in boiling water is all it takes.

(You may, however, need to pretend that the eggs in fresh pasta have been voluntarily donated by free range hens in the interest of better spaghetti.)

Dried pasta simply needs bunging in boiling salted water for about 8 minutes. Many of the 'saucier' recipes in this book can be poured onto or mixed with cooked spaghetti, macaroni, shells, whirls or shapes.

DEEP FRYING

Forget the shock horror stories you may have heard. Deep frying is perfectly safe and easy. Good commercial vegetable oil contains an anti-spattering agent to keep you from frying with the chips.

Invest in a big chip pan and keep it *half* filled with vegetable oil. The oil will see you through for months without needing a change. Just top it up occasionally and keep it covered with a lid when you're not using it.

Put the pan on a medium heat and leave it (under supervision) for 5 minutes. Make sure that whatever you're frying is as dry as possible. Select one item and drop it in. If it sizzles and floats, send in the troops (gently).

It's always better to fry a few things at a time in batches. Also safer! The more you try and do at one go, the longer it takes. Drain the finished items on some kitchen roll. DON'T FORGET TO TURN OFF THE HEAT WHEN YOU'VE FINISHED.

Besides the obvious chips, try deep fried whole carrots, chopped turnips, TVP sausages, *drained* canned potatoes, frozen new potatoes, whole mushrooms (frozen or fresh), frozen onion rings, etc.

Now we've got the traditional plate fillers out of the way, let's move straight into the world of international cookery . . .

5

Throughout the initial sections of this publication, we have established the fundamental requirements for culinary productivity. Henceforth, and to the exclusion of any diversification, we shall endeavour to explore a cornucopia of sundry delicacies. They will be primarily of a savoury nature, culled from the folklore and customs of our international heritage. Due modification has been made, where necessary, to enable the full benefit of contemporary technology to be exploited in the preparation of the aforementioned, thus allowing maximum speed and efficiency.

Or, to put it another way, hang on to your hats and prepare to go

AROUND THE WORLD WITH A CAN OPENER . . .

A CULINARY TRAVELOGUE

MARSEILLE

RATATOUILLE VARIATIONS

(serves 2)

Here is a secret recipe which has been handed down in our family from generation to generation. Ratatouille is a delightful French dish of mixed courgettes, aubergines, onions and tomatoes. Its subtle flavour comes from a delicate blend of herbs, spices and olive oil. You can buy a can of it in any reputable supermarket.

1 can vegetable ratatouille
several thin slices of cheese
4 slices of bread (any colour but green)
butter or margarine

You need a pan with a lid and a grill or toaster.

1 Heat the ratatouille slowly on a medium heat.

2 Stir it when it begins to bubble.

3 Put the cheese slices on top.

4 Cover with lid.

5 Toast and butter the bread.

6 Pour the ratatouille on the toast.

7 Eat it!

NB There are two schools of thought on this recipe. Those who dislike soggy toast may prefer to put the cheese on the toast instead of on the ratatouille.

MUSHROOM RATATOUILLE

(serves 2)

*ingredients as before, **plus** 4 oz fresh mushrooms and a little margarine*

1 Put a little margarine in a saucepan and place on a medium heat.

2 Give the mushrooms a quick rinse and wipe dry.

3 When the marge starts to sizzle, sling in the mushrooms . . . whole!

4 Shake the pan over the heat for a minute or so.

5 Add the ratatouille and carry on as before.

Instead of toast, you could serve this with rice.

By now you must be getting the idea. The recipes in this book are not supposed to be followed religiously. They are ideas which may serve to inspire the creative cook. (That's you!) Of course, if you *do* follow them to the letter, they'll work. But if, for example, you haven't got all the ingredients, feel free to *improvise*.

le left Bank

CHAMPIGNONS À LA CARTE

(serves 2)

This is French for mushrooms 'on the map'. Personally, I prefer them on the plate! Mushrooms are easy. All they need is a quick rinse and wipe. You don't even need to chop them. Just break them into pieces.

1 clove le garlic (optional)
1 oz margarine
8 oz fresh mushrooms
1 can condensed mushroom soup
oregano
cream

1 Peel the clove of garlic (a clove is one segment, *not* the whole bulb) and chop it into tiny pieces.

2 Give it a quick sauté. (This is a posh way of saying fry it in some marge on a medium heat.) Then break up the mushrooms and sling them in.

3 Shake the pan about for a minute or two. When the mushrooms begin to shrink, add the soup, oregano and a dollop* of cream. Stir enthusiastically.

4 Serve on toast, on a bed of rice, with chips, or let it cool and use it in a sandwich!

* A dollop is somewhere between a few drops and the whole tub.

I wanted to include a recipe for vegetarian frogs legs - but I couldn't find a vegetarian frog!

MUSHROOM SOUP

(serves 2)

As above till you get to the last bit, then fill the empty soup can with milk and tip it in. Stir till boiling and serve with a packet of croûtons.

RISOTTO
(serves 2)

For maximum ethnic effect, turn up the central heating, put on your swimsuit and eat this dish to the sound of Edmundo Ross records!

8 oz rice
½ head of celery
1 tablespoon oil
4 oz frozen onions
1 small can sweetcorn
4 oz frozen peas
1 small can tomatoes
a few pinches of herbs
paprika
Cheddar cheese

1 Boil the rice (see p. 18).

2 Meanwhile, thinly slice the celery and sauté in the oil with the onions in a *large* frying pan for a few minutes.

3 Shove in the drained sweetcorn, peas, herbs (oregano, marjoram and parsley would be good) and tomatoes (include the liquid). Simmer gently till the rice is cooked.

4 Drain the rice and turn into the frying pan, a bit at a time, stirring it in as you go. Keep stirring or it'll stick. Shower with paprika and grated cheese and serve.

If you let it go cold, you can pretend it's a salad and serve it with lettuce.

CAULIFLOWER CHEESE

(serves 4)

This dish is invariably served by meat-eaters to their vegetarian friends. I've never actually met anyone who likes it, but just in case you've acquired the taste, here's the recipe!

1 lb frozen cauliflower florets
1 packet cheese sauce mix
milk or water as required

Sling the florets in ½ inch of S.B.W. and simmer for 8 mins. Make up the sauce mix as per packet, and pour over the drained cauli.

SICILY

MACARONI BAKE

(serves 4)

1 big can macaroni cheese
1 big can sweetcorn
mixed herbs as preferred
8 oz mushrooms
6 oz Cheddar cheese
baking dish

Turn oven up to warm.

Put the macaroni and sweetcorn in baking dish and mix together with the herbs. Slice mushrooms and lay them on top. Slice (or grate) cheese and lay on top of that. Pop in the middle of the oven. Wait 30 minutes and serve.

Goes well with oven chips (simply place in the oven at the same time on a higher shelf) and a salad.

Macaroni is great if you're on a diet...

...just eat the holes in the middle !!!

FETTUCINE ALLA CREMA

(serves 2)

Fettucine is spaghetti that's been run over by a steamroller. It looks a bit like tangled shoelaces, but it tastes much better.

8 oz fettucine or tagliatelle
salt
1 clove garlic, chopped
4 oz mushrooms, sliced
1 oz butter
1 pack frozen spinach
mixed herbs
4 oz frozen peas
small carton single cream
2 oz grated mozzarella cheese ← *oh alright then... EDAM will do!*

Some people thaw spinach by putting it in the airing cupboard for a few hours. I find it melts all over the towels. A quicker way is to pop it in a frying pan with a little butter on a low heat and turn it after 5 minutes.

Fill a saucepan with boiling water and throw in the fettu-thingamy with a pinch of salt. Let it boil away merrily while you fry up the garlic and mushrooms in some butter. When the mushrooms begin to shrink, throw in the spinach and mixed herbs. Stir vigorously for a while. Hurl in the peas, stir some more and then chuck in the cream.

The noodles should be done by now. Put them on a plate, cover with the sauce and top with grated cheese.

For extra finesse, stick the finished plates under the grill for a minute.

LASAGNA ASPARAGI

(serves 2)

This recipe calls for lasagna and asparagus tips. I don't have any tips for asparagus but I have a lasagna tip. The so-called 'instant' sort doesn't work. (Unless you like eating cardboard.)

8 oz lasagna
1 can condensed asparagus soup
1 can asparagus
8 oz sliced mushrooms
grated cheese

1 Turn the oven on to medium.

2 Boil the lasagna in a big saucepan, according to instructions on the packet. When it's cooked, lift it out and use 4 pieces to line a baking dish.

3 Put half the asparagi on top, cover with half the soup, top with half the mushrooms. Now repeat the whole process again. Finish with the lasagna and top with grated cheese.

4 Shove in the oven for 30 minutes and serve.

ROMA

SPAGHETTI NAPOLITAN
(serves 2–3)

The complicated thing about this dish is not cooking it, but eating it.

8 oz long spaghetti (cooking instructions should be on the packet)

1 can tomato spaghetti sauce (not Bolognese, that's meat)

4 oz Parmesan cheese (Go on, buy it fresh and grate it yourself!)

Use an enormous saucepan two-thirds full of boiling salted water. Put as much spaghetti as you can in the pan and after a few moments it will subside, allowing you to drop in the rest. Give it a light stir and let it boil fiercely while you heat the sauce. Drain the spaghetti and pour on the sauce. Serve with a spoon, fork and full protective clothing! (And don't forget to sprinkle on the Parmesan.)

ATHENS

SPINACH SURPRISE

(serves 4)

This recipe goes down well with Olive Oil (and her friend)!

**1 small can cut green beans
8 oz frozen spinach
8 oz broccoli (fresh if in season)
4 oz frozen onions
1 1-pint packet spring vegetable soup
butter or margarine
1 small carton cottage cheese**

 1 Put a large pan on a low heat. Pour in the liquid from the green beans. Drop in the spinach, cover and simmer for 5 mins. Chop the broccoli into tiny pieces if fresh (don't bother if frozen) and sling it in the pan. Give it about 4 minutes of simmering and stirring.

2 Add the frozen onions and the packet soup about now. Stir and simmer for 4 minutes more. Add the green beans and butter. More simmering, more stirring.

3 When you get bored, pour it on to a bed of rice, noodles, or mashed potatoes. Top with cottage cheese, so the plate looks like a green and white Mexican's hat, viewed from above. Decorate with a sprig of parsley, some strands of cress or a few leaves off the pot plant of your choice!

WARSAW STUFFED PEPPERS

(serves 2)

You can use any sort of pepper for this recipe, except greaseproof.

*2 large peppers
1 can aubergines in tomato sauce*

Turn the oven on to medium. Slice the peppers in half. Carve out the seeds and throw 'em away. Put the peppers on a baking tray and stuff the empty shells with the canned aubergines. Bake for 20 minutes.

Budapest

POTATO GOULASH

(serves 2)

This dish comes from Hungary. *(I hope you are!)*

1 big can new potatoes
1 pack goulash mix
8 oz frozen mixed vegetables
1 small carton sour cream

1 Pour the potatoes with the liquid into a saucepan. Leave for 2 minutes on a lowish heat.

2 Add the goulash mix, stir well.

3 7 minutes later, add mixed veg. Keep stirring for 2–3 minutes.

4 Add sour cream and serve.

CHICAGO

STUFFED POTATOES

(serves 4)

4 big potatoes, pre-washed
8 oz cottage cheese
1 small can sweetcorn
plenty of fresh parsley

1 Rinse the potatoes and stick them on the top shelf of a hot oven for an hour.

2 Go to the library and take back those overdue books.

3 Come back, take out the potatoes and slice in half.

4 Scoop out most of the flesh into a mixing bowl. Add the other ingredients, chopping the parsley very fine. Mix well and shove back in the potato skins. It won't fit, of course, unless you pile it high!

5 Put them all back in the oven for 20 minutes while you start one of your new books.

POTATO SKINS

(serves 2)

**3 lbs large pre-washed potatoes
1 large tub sour cream
deep-frying equipment**

1 Rinse the potatoes and bake them as above. Let them cool down and slice in quarters. This time, try to keep the flesh inside whole as you carve it out. Deep fry the skins (see page 19) and serve them with a sour cream dip.

2 Deep fry the flesh as chips and try to get them to the table before you eat them. *(This is not easy!)*

MEXICAN TACOS

(serves 3–4)

This is a vegetarian version of an authentic Mexican treat. After a few tequilas, you won't even miss the meat!

**1 can kidney beans
1 packet taco flavouring
1 packet tacos
lettuce
Edam cheese, grated
1 packet taco sauce**

1 Turn on the oven, high.

2 Pour the kidney beans into a bowl, liquid and all. Add the taco flavouring. Mash it to a stodgy pulp.

3 Spoon into the taco shells till each is half full. Lay them carefully on an ovenproof plate and pop in the oven.

4 Five minutes later pull them out, shouting authentic Mexican things like *Olé* and *Ariba*. Top with shredded lettuce, grated cheese and lashings of taco sauce.

Serve with Guacamole (see Salads).

CANTON
ORIENTAL SOPHISTICATION
(serves 2)

This is your actual stir-fry recipe. The soy sauce should really be the expensive stuff, called *Shoyu*, which you get in health stores. It's noticeably nicer.

8 oz small carrots
½ Chinese leaf (in season) or ½ a small white cabbage
2 tablespoons oil
8 oz frozen onions
8 oz fresh mushrooms
1 can bamboo shoots, drained
8 oz fresh beansprouts
soy sauce
pepper

1 The carrots and Chinese leaf need chopping quite fine.

2 Fry them over a high heat in the oil. Stir and shake it about a lot.

3 After about 3 minutes, add the frozen onions.

4 Two minutes later, add the mushrooms, broken into chunks, and *drained* bamboo shoots. Reduce heat to low. Stir and cover.

5 After 2 minutes stir in the beansprouts and keep stirring until they go soft (not too soft).

6 Just before serving, adds LOTS of soy sauce and LOTS of black pepper.

Serve with rice and chopsticks. Bring to the table muttering, 'It will further the superior man to cook the great dinner.'

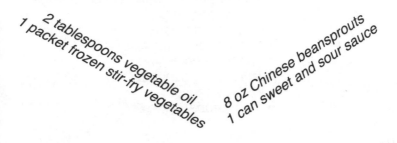

Peking

INSTANT CHINESE MEAL
(or Suey Chop Chop)

(serves 2)

Culinary purists like to cook this sort of food in a wok. It helps create an oriental atmosphere. If you haven't got one, just use a large frying pan and slant your eyes!

2 tablespoons vegetable oil
1 packet frozen stir-fry vegetables

8 oz Chinese beansprouts
1 can sweet and sour sauce

1 Heat the oil in velly hot pan. Add honourable stir-fly vegetables. Shake well.

2 Add beansplouts straight from packet (unless they've been sitting around for a day or two, in which case give 'em a quick rinse). Shake even weller.

3 Pour in can of sweet and sour sauce, let it simmer on a lower heat for a couple of minutes.

Serve with soggy rice or overcooked noodles. Bring to table proclaiming, 'One Number Flourty-two to take away.'

POONA

CURRY

(serves 2)

Like a Turkish bath, a good curry should bring you out in a sweat! However, it is not advisable to sit in a curry!

8 oz frozen mixed vegetables
4 oz frozen onions
lots of butter
1 can curry sauce (choose from mild, medium and ouch)

Fry the veg in the butter. Throw in the sauce, stir, simmer and serve with . . .

DELHI MUSHROOM BYRIANI

(serves 2)

A dish similar to this can be had in every 'Taj Mahal' and 'Star of India' between Bradford and Brixton. If you think it takes a long time to cook, remember how long it takes to attract the attention of a waiter in these places!

1 can precooked rice
8 oz mushrooms
1 tablespoon curry paste or byriani paste

Cook the rice as per instructions. Fry the mushrooms, stir into the cooked rice, add the curry paste and serve with the curry.

Goes well with popadoms (you grill them *very quickly*) and raitta (see Salads).

BRUSSELS SPROUTS IN PEANUT BUTTER SAUCE

(serves 2)

I know this sounds odd, but it tastes great. Use the nice commercial peanut butter, not those ground-up iron filings they sell in health stores.

1 lb frozen Brussels sprouts
1 can condensed celery soup
½ soup can of milk/water
2 tablespoons peanut butter
soy sauce

Pop the sprouts in a pan with ¼ inch of boiling salted water. Cover and simmer on a low heat for 5 minutes, then drain well. Heat the celery soup while stirring in the milk/water and peanut butter. Keep stirring, it *will* dissolve! Mix in the soy sauce just before serving and pour over the sprouts.

FALAFEL AND HUMMOUS IN PITTA

(serves 3)

You *ought* to wash your hands before you start this recipe. You'll *have* to wash your hands when you've finished it!

1 pack falafel mix
1 packet pitta bread
1 can hummous
½ lettuce (shredded)
2 tomatoes (sliced)
pickled chilli peppers
deep-frying equipment

1 Follow the instructions on the falafel mix. It is important to measure the amount of water you use. Shape into little balls and deep fry. Fish 'em out when they turn golden and drain on a piece of kitchen roll.

a guessing!!

2 Warm the pitta bread for a few seconds under the grill. Split it open like they do in the kebab restaurants. Spread the hummous inside and stuff with salad and falafels. Top with a pickled chilli pepper.

CHICKPEAS AND ONIONS

(serves 2)

In the USA they call these garbanzo beans. They also call marrows squash, car boots trunks and Benny Hill funny. Odd people the Americans.

4 oz frozen baby onions
margarine or butter
1 can cooked chickpeas
any herbs or spices you have to hand (oregano, parsley, garlic, mixed herbs or curry powder)

Fry the onions in the butter or margarine for about 4 minutes. Bung in the drained chickpeas and the herbs and spices. Fry vigorously for 5 minutes more. Eat with apéritif. Or even a whole set of them.

BELSIZE PARK, N.W.3

TOMATO BRUNCH

(serves 1)

I eat this on Sunday mornings. It always cures my hangover, but that could be because of the six cups of black coffee I wash it down with.

8 oz ripe tomatoes
8 oz sliced mushrooms
butter
lots of fresh parsley
oregano
salt and pepper

Quarter the tomatoes and fry them with the mushrooms in the butter for 3 minutes over a brisk heat. Stir constantly. Add the herbs and carry on for 2 more minutes.
Serve with cheese on toast. *(and the colour supplement !)*

6
COMMERCIAL BREAKS

THE ULTIMATE IN TV DINNERS

Have you ever arrived home, starving hungry and yet anxious to watch something on TV? Well, here are some meals you can cook during the commercial breaks . . . I've designed them for programmes that last an hour with two breaks. If, where you live, there are more breaks or you want to watch a programme that's longer, you'll have to adapt the recipe yourself.

The astute reader may have noticed on the cover a claim that no recipe in this book will take more than 20 minutes to make. This is in fact a lie. The following recipes all take at least an hour *but*, as the total amount of preparation time is well under 10 minutes . . . it's not so much a lie as an elaboration on the truth. And what is truth anyway? I mean, can we really say that ANYTHING is true? I mean, surely it's all relative . . . After all, isn't life an illusion? A series of apparently connected events with no bearing on reality other than the connections we perceive and assume to be verifiable???

(yawn...)

COMMERCIAL BREAK 1

BAKED POTATOES, VEGETABLES, PIZZA AND ASPARAGUS SAUCE

(serves 2)

2 large pre-washed potatoes
8 oz cabbage, cauliflower or broccoli (frozen or fresh)
1 can condensed asparagus soup
1 big dollop of cream or 2 small glugs of milk
1 clove garlic, finely chopped
butter and cheese to taste
1 small frozen pizza

JUST BEFORE THE SHOW . . .

Turn the oven pretty high. Shove the potatoes on to a high shelf, giving them a quick rinse first if you're fussy. Don't worry about all that 'pre-heated oven' rubbish. That stuff only really matters for cakes. The rest of the time, it's just something cookery book writers say to worry their readers.

IN THE FIRST COMMERCIAL BREAK
(about 15–20 minutes later)

Return to the kitchen. Open the oven and pierce the potatoes with a fork (to avoid potential explosion). If you're cooking a *fresh* vegetable, this is when you rinse it and slice it if necessary. Fill the kettle and boil it (or leave a pan of water on a low heat if your kettle doesn't turn itself off). Find a baking tray for the pizza. Open the can of asparagus soup and pour it into a small oven dish. Add a dollop of cream or milk and the garlic, finely chopped. Stir together. DON'T start anything else cooking yet! Return to your cosy chair in front of the tele.

IN THE SECOND COMMERCIAL BREAK
(15–20 minutes later)

Once more, the kitchen awaits you! Put the pizza on the tray and dump it in the middle of the oven. (Remember to unwrap it!) Pop the bowl with the asparagus sauce on the bottom shelf of the oven. Pour the boiled water from your kettle into a large saucepan and put it on a low heat. Chuck in the prepared vegetables. Return once more to your cosy chair.

AT THE END OF THE SHOW . . .
(15 minutes later)

Fish out the vegetables and drain them (they should be just pleasantly overcooked). Bung 'em on a plate. Now extract the contents of the oven (USE AN OVEN GLOVE FOR PETE'S SAKE) and dish them out too. Pour the sauce over the vegetables and potatoes. Serve with butter and grated cheese. Settle back down in your cosy chair and watch the news while you're eating.

By now, you will have noticed a fatal flaw in this 'instant TV dinner' business. If you haven't got the ingredients to hand, there's nothing instant about it. The answer, of course, is to move home. Every committed Junk Food Vegetarian should live next door to a 24-hour supermarket. The only alternative is to work on the 'mountain to Mohammed' principle. Become a Hobbit. Turn your kitchen cupboard into a veritable treasure trove of edible delights. Visit a supermarket once a week – or once a month – and purchase large quantities of every can, packet and vegetable that catches your eye. Stagger home with your spoils in a taxi. I know it sounds like a painfully grown-up way of shopping, but there's a great advantage to it: once you have crammed your cupboards, stuffed your shelves and filled your freezer, you can sit back and relax – secure in the knowledge that instant gourmet meals are available at any time of the day or night.

To help you digest this information, here's a sort of Shepherd's Pie without the Shepherd.

VEGETABLE PIE WITH SALAD

(serves 2)

4 oz frozen onions
6 oz frozen mixed vegetables
1 can condensed celery soup
1 can imitation steaks (optional)
spices, garlic, etc, to taste
2 cans boiled potatoes
1 fresh tomato, chopped
4 oz cheese
butter

SALAD
½ small red or green cabbage
1 or 2 pickled beetroots
3 big squirts lemon juice
1 small packet dry roasted peanuts
4 oz raisins
salt and pepper and oregano
1 teaspoon vinegar
1 teaspoon oil

BEFORE THE SHOW . . .

Slice up the cabbage small, slice up the beetroot chunky, mix all salad ingredients together in a large bowl. Leave to conglomerate! Turn on the oven to medium. (This is one occasion when a pre-heated oven helps matters.)

FIRST COMMERCIAL BREAK

Get a large oven dish (casserole type). Mix together the veggies and soup (plus 'steak' if desired). Add spices and seasoning to taste (garlic, herbs, etc). Cover dish and shove in oven on the middle shelf. Open cans of potato and mash them as shown on p. 18, but cold.

SECOND COMMERCIAL BREAK

Open oven, pull out casserole dish. Take off lid and spoon mashed potato on top. DON'T COVER the dish this time when you put it back in the oven. Grate the cheese in anticipation of . . .

END OF SHOW . . .

Open oven. The potato should be crisping on top. Cover with cheese and shove back in for 5 minutes till cheese bubbles. Meanwhile, lay the table, dish out the salad and/or prepare a dessert.

7

IT TASTES LIKE MEAT TO ME

THE SINCEREST FORM OF FLATTERY?

Once a nut roast was the closest a vegetarian could get to a T-bone steak.

Meat, despite its unsavoury origins, has a chewiness that the plant kingdom fails to supply. Now, thanks to the wonders of science, it's possible to have the pleasure without the guilt!!! The wisdom of nature and the magic of new technology have combined to give us processed soya.

Soya beans are staggeringly good for you. They are also staggeringly boring. However, when cooked to a very high temperature and forced through a stainless steel mesh they gain a texture that resembles meat. Using flavouring of vegetable origin, it is possible to give them a 'meaty' taste, too.

Although few soya products would fool a committed carnivore, it's amazing how they can worry a vegetarian. Even I sometimes have to read the packet to reassure myself! Even if YOU don't like the idea, your meat-eating dinner guests may appreciate it. Children also tend to like it.

There are new variations coming on to the market all the time. Not all are made from soya. Nuts and wheat are also used.

The recipes below are based on the products that I know can be found. Unfortunately, few supermarkets stock them. Texturised Vegetable Protein (TVP) is one of the few things a Junk Food Vegetarian needs to go to a health shop for.

As a rule of thumb, there are two sorts. Packets (just add water) and cans (heat and serve). At the time of writing, the first frozen TVP is appearing in the shops. An asterisk implies that you can find it in frozen form, too.

We'll start with Frankfurters (*).

HOT DOGS

(serves 4)

This popular item is often eaten in cinemas. To re-create an authentic atmosphere at home, draw the curtains, put on a video and stub your cigarettes out on the carpet!

1 can TVP frankfurters*
4 oz frozen onions
oil for frying
8 hot dog rolls
mustard and/or ketchup

Drain the frankfurters and fry them with the onions in a little oil. Pop the rolls in a warm oven. When the onions are soft, open the rolls and pop a hot dog in each one. Top with a few onions and pour on the ketchup. Yum-Yum.

FRANKS AND BROCCOLI

(serves 4)

4 oz frozen onions
8 oz fresh or frozen broccoli
1 clove garlic
8 oz sliced mushrooms
1 can TVP frankfurters*
fresh parsley
8 oz Edam cheese

1. Fry the onions and broccoli in a *large* pan. If the broccoli is fresh, chop off the bottom ⅓ of the stalks and throw away.
2. Stir and sizzle for 4 minutes and add the chopped garlic, mushrooms and drained franks, chopped in half. Reduce the heat, stir and cover.
3. Leave for 4 minutes more, shaking the pan occasionally.
4. Open the lid and cover with *plenty* of finely chopped parsley and thinly sliced (or grated) cheese. *Do not stir*. Cover again and leave for 3 minutes or until the cheese is fully melted.
5. Use a flat spatula to serve with chips or rice.

IMITATION STEAKS

Not for the squeamish! They bring to mind striped aprons and straw boaters – and yet, they are 100% vegetable. You'll find them in cans (with tasty gravy), or in packets (dehydrated with complex soaking instructions). Don't throw away the packaging – you may need it for reassurance when you sink your teeth into these chewy, fleshy, visceral items.

Fry them, grill them, or try a canful in a casserole . . . with 8 oz of frozen Brussels sprouts and 4 oz frozen peas. Sling the whole lot in a covered dish and place on the bottom shelf of a hot oven – while roasting 1 lb of potatoes for 40 minutes on the top shelf. Serves 4 brave vegetarians!

Or try . . .

CHINESE DELIGHT

(serves 2)

1 can imitation steak
4 sticks celery
8 oz Chinese beansprouts
4 oz frozen onions
8 oz frozen green beans
10 whole black peppercorns
soy sauce
a little oil

Drain the can of 'steak' and save the gravy. Slice the bits into thin strips and do the same with the celery. Stir fry ALL the ingredients in a little oil for 8 minutes. Just before you stop, pour on the gravy with a good shake of soy sauce.

Leave the black peppers in. I dare you to eat them!

← This is Chinese for : "Your cheque is in the post !"

SOSMIX

Now available from enlightened supermarkets as well as from the so-called health stores, this stuff is invaluable for a Junk Food Vegetarian. Unlike many other TVP products, it is not overly meaty or strong in taste – yet, if shaped into sausages, its pink colour and texture give a passing imitation of bangers.

Supplied dry, in bags or packets, the stuff itself is a strange mixture of powder and granules. Add water, stir, wait about 5 minutes and . . . you have the most wonderful material for baking, deep or shallow frying, boiling or grilling. You can make it into patties, balls, sausages, loaves or even pancakes!* It cooks in next to no time.

Just one word of advice. For some reason, the manufacturers seem to underestimate the amount of water you need to add to it. Ignore what it says on the packet – add about 10% more! Actually, it's pretty impossible to add too much water (unless you go really wild). You'll just give it a softer texture.

* For pancakes, make it very wet indeed and use like pancake mix!

SAUSAGE, BEANS AND CHIPS

(serves 4)

1 13-oz packet Sosmix
1 lb oven chips
butter
1 large can baked beans

1. Turn on the oven (high).
2. Make up the Sosmix and wait for it to set.
3. Lay the chips on a tray and pop in the oven.
4. Shape the sausage mix by rolling it in your hands. This is a bit sticky but warm water soon removes the stickiness.
5. Fry the sausages on a medium heat in a little butter, turning after 3 minutes.
6. Heat up the beans.

OR

Use real chips and *deep* fry the sausages. They cook much quicker that way.

ROAST LOAF

(serves 4)

1 13-oz pack Sosmix
4 oz sliced mushrooms
½ onion, finely chopped (yes . . . a fresh one, tears and all!)
fresh chopped parsley

1. Turn on the oven (high).
2. Pour the Sosmix into a casserole dish and add the recommended quantity of water plus half as much again. Stir it (no need to wait) and then stir in all other ingredients.
3. Pop in the oven for 30 minutes and, with any luck, it should turn out of its dish like a loaf and be sliceable!

This can also be served cold. Stand in the refrigerator for 20 minutes and when cold enough come out and serve it.

SOSODUMPLING SOUP

(serves 4)

½ 13-oz pack Sosmix
1 packet dried spring vegetable soup

Form the Sosmix into little balls, about 1 inch in diameter. Make up the soup as per packet and when it starts to boil pop in your sosodumplings. They'll be done when the soup's cooked.

STUFFED MARROW

(serves 4)

1 large marrow
1 13-oz pack Sosmix

1. Chop the marrow into 4-inch slices. Simmer in plenty of salted boiling water for 5 minutes.
2. Make up the Sosmix. Pull out the marrow and, using a sharp knife, cut out a wide circle around the seeds and throw the middle away. Lay on a greased baking tray, stuff with Sosmix, and pop in a medium oven for 20 minutes.

SIZZLES

. . . are like Sosmix with pieces of imitation smoky bacon mixed in. If you can't buy them in your area, make your own by purchasing the imitation bacon bits. See below.

SCRAMBLED SIZZLES

½ 13-oz pack of Sizzles
margarine
4 oz frozen onions
4 oz frozen peas

Make up the Sizzles as per pack. Fry the onion in some margarine. As it begins to soften, add the peas and Sizzles. Don't form it into patties. Stir it around and let it break up in the pan. Keep doing this till you get tired (about 5 minutes).
   Serve with beans on toast.

IMITATION BACON BITS

You can sometimes buy these at the herb and spice rack in a supermarket. Otherwise, I'm afraid it's a 'health' store. You can add them to just about everything – including salads.

BURGAMIX

This is similar in principle to Sosmix. Exactly the same comments apply with regards to making it up.

CHEESEBURGERS

(serves 4)

1 13-oz pack Burgamix
oil
1–2 onions, sliced
8 sesame burger buns
8 slices processed cheese
mustard, pickle or ketchup to taste

1. Make up the Burgamix, let it set and form into large, burger shaped patties.
2. Fry them in a little oil with the onions. Turn with a spatula after 4 minutes.
3. Warm the buns in the oven, shove in the burgers, pop the cheese on top and eat with relish!

PITTABURGERS

(serves 4)

1 13-oz pack Burgamix
1 pack of pitta bread
4 oz mixed veg
8 oz whole button mushrooms
8 oz Edam cheese
relish or mustard

1. Shape the Burgamix to match the size of the pitta bread.
2. Fry it as before with the veg and mushrooms.
3. Slice the cheese.
4. When both sides of the burger are cooked, lay the cheese on top, reduce the heat and cover the pan.
5. Warm the pitta under the grill for a few seconds on each side.
6. Slice pitta open lengthways and slide the knife inside to form a pocket. Spread a little relish on the bottom of the pocket.
7. Carefully transfer the patties into the pitta, using a spatula, and share out the veggies between each one. Eat with your hands. ← AND your mouth !!

BURGALOAF

Make up the Burgamix in a bread tin or casserole dish. Use half as much *more* water than it says on the pack. Pop straight in a medium oven and leave for 30 minutes. Slice, and serve with boiled potatoes and gravy. (Make the gravy by using Bisto and the water from the canned boiled potatoes.)

TACOS

See the taco recipe earlier in the book. Instead of mashed kidney beans, add the taco seasoning to 1 13-oz pack of Burgamix and make up with a little extra water. It works out just right.

SOYAMINCE

This comes flavoured or unflavoured. Personally, I prefer the blander version. The simplest way to deal with it is 1 cup of boiling water to 1 cup of soya mince. Don't bother cooking, just mix in a bowl, add a teaspoonful of oil and leave for 10 minutes. There are a thousand and one uses including:

SPAGHETTI BOLOGNESE

Make as per the recipe on page 27 but add 2 cups of made-up mince to the can of sauce and stir while you simmer.

CURRIED MINCE

1 packet curry sauce
4 oz frozen onions
4 oz frozen peas
2 cups made-up mince

Mix the curry sauce with ¼ pint of cold water. Pour it in a pan, sling in all other ingredients, cover and simmer on a low heat for 12 minutes.

STUFFED COURGETTES

... otherwise known as a 'zucchini' (which sounds like a swimsuit you wear at the zoo). Also known (in the USA) as a 'zucchini squash'... presumably a tight fitting version of the same thing!

1 lb large courgettes
8 oz frozen spinach
1 small can sweetcorn
2 cups made-up mince
lots of whatever cheese is to hand

1. Slice the courgettes in half lengthways. Using a sharp knife, carve out a hollow. Throw away the middles and lay the courgettes on a baking tray.
2. Thaw the spinach (see recipe p. 25) and mix with the drained sweetcorn and mince.
3. Stuff the courgettes with the mixture and let the rest flow gracefully over the edges and on to the baking tray. Pop in a medium oven for 20 minutes.
4. Grate cheese over the top just before serving.

SOYA CHUNKS

... are not quick – and anyway I don't like them. Feel free to experiment, though, and FOLLOW THE INSTRUCTIONS ON THE PACKET about simmering in water and a little oil for at least 10 minutes.

TOFU

Tofu is the oldest form of TVP in the world. It dates back to ancient China and is a sort of 'soya cheese' that you fry! In England it can only really be bought at a reasonable price from Chinese supermarkets and it's worth the trip.

There are two sorts, raw and ready-fried. Although there's a recipe for raw tofu in the salad chapter, I recommend the ready-fried variety for cooking.

Here's a simple recipe . . .

1 can condensed tomato soup
1 teaspoon Marmite
8 pieces of ready-fried tofu

Put the soup in a casserole dish. Fill the empty can half-full with boiling water and dissolve the Marmite in it. Mix in with the soup and stir in the tofu. It will try to float so just coat it well, stick on a lid and bung it in a medium oven for 40 minutes.

You can also add ready-fried tofu to any sauce or stir-fry meal. Pop it in quite early on and let it soak up the flavour of whatever it's cooking with.

8

WHAT'S FOR PUDDING?

SWEET, SWEET SURRENDER

Once I found myself trapped for a weekend with 150 members of the 'consciousness revolution'. It was the long hot summer of '76 and against my better judgment I had agreed to attend a spiritual 'retreat'. An endless chain of seminars and workshops was finally broken by the call for dinner. I didn't flinch when it turned out to be bulgar and buckwheat. 'Perhaps,' I thought, 'suffering is good for the soul.'

The dessert *looked* like apple crumble and custard. It tasted like old socks and shaving foam. Determined to find an explanation, I stormed towards the kitchen where my path was blocked by a girl wearing a cheesecloth smock and a benign expression.

'We aren't serving second helpings yet,' she said firmly.

'Oh that's all right,' I replied, my voice heavy with sarcasm. 'I just wondered if you could give me the recipe.'

Her face lit up in a glow of pride. 'Oh, well, the custard is made with milk and soya flour . . .'

'There isn't much sugar in it,' I muttered.

'There isn't ANY sugar in it,' she replied proudly. 'The sweetness comes naturally from the apples and adzuki beans.'

'Adzuki beans?'

'Adzuki beans,' she beamed. 'It's Apple and Adzuki bean crumble.'

I suppose it is a tribute to the power of mind over matter. You'd have to be highly evolved to swallow that sort of thing. For those of us still drowning in the sea of illusion, the following recipes are lovingly dedicated.

ALL RECIPES IN THIS SECTION ARE FOR 4 MODERATE EATERS, OR 2 HUNGRY PEOPLE

or ONE greedy pig !!

APPLE CRUMBLE AND CUSTARD

WARNING: This recipe calls for gratuitous violence!

4 oz plain biscuits
2 oz warm, softened butter
1 tablespoon milk
1 can apple pie filling
1 can custard

1. Turn the oven on to medium.
2. Put the biscuits in a strong paper bag. Run backwards and forwards over the bag with a steam roller, or attack it with a blunt instrument until you have lots of tiny pieces of broken biscuit. Alternatively, use a polythene bag. Tie a knot in the top and smash mercilessly against a brick wall!
3. Mix the biscuit crumbs with the butter and milk. Empty the pie filling into a casserole dish and cover with the biscuits.
4. Shove the whole lot in the oven for 20 minutes.
5. If you can't be bothered to cook the custard in a pan, pour it in a bowl and bake it on the bottom shelf of the same oven for the same length of time.

APPLE SPONGE

Here is a real opportunity to show off your versatility. Simply by substituting rhubarb, blackberry or apricot pie filling, a whole new world of possibilities opens up.

1 pack sponge cake mix
1 can apple pie filling

Turn the oven on high. Make up the sponge mixture as per packet. Don't add the egg unless you eat eggs! Just add 2 extra tablespoons of milk. Empty the pie filling into a casserole dish, pour on the mixture and bake for 20 minutes.

BANANA SPLIT

This recipe calls for whipped cream. No Junk Food Vegetarian should be without a can of this in the fridge. You simply squirt it on to *any* dessert and it adds class. Incidentally, it's kept under pressure with nitrous oxide which is LAUGHING GAS. If you haven't found the jokes in this book funny yet, read the rest of it with a can of whipped cream up your nose.

1 small can chocolate sauce
2 ripe bananas
1 small pack, Cornish ice cream
wafers or biscuits
1 can instant whipped cream

Heat the chocolate sauce. It's messy but you could avoid this by cooking it in the can (see p. 13). Slice the bananas in half, lengthways. Pop them on a plate and sandwich the ice cream between them. Pour on the chocolate sauce and decorate with wafers. Smother in whipped cream.

BANANA CUSTARD

1 ripe banana
1 can custard
1 handful sultanas
cinnamon

Slice the banana into medium pieces and mix all ingredients in a saucepan. Heat and eat!

BANANA FLAMBÉ

2 oz butter
2 firm bananas
1 orange
4 tablespoons brandy

Melt the butter in a frying pan. Slice the bananas in half, lengthways, and fry gently in the butter. Turn after a minute. Squeeze the orange and pour all the juice into the pan. When all is bubbling and sizzling, pour on the brandy and set light to it. Bring to the table in a blaze of glory!

(Note: if you're not into brandy, don't buy a whole bottle. Use a miniature.)

FRUIT SALAD

1 ripe pear
1 apple
2 bananas
2 oranges
1 can pineapple chunks
1 can peach slices
8 oz fresh or frozen strawberries

Slice the pear, apple and bananas into smallish chunks. Juice both oranges and mix with EVERYTHING else in a large bowl. Leave for 3 hours. Do something sensual to work up an appetite while you're waiting. Serve with whipped cream. *(if you've got any left by then!)*

RICE AND FRUIT PUDDING

**1 apple or pear
1 can rice pudding
4 oz sultanas
cinnamon
nutmeg**

Turn the oven on to medium. Chop the apple or pear into little pieces, and mix with everything else. Pop in a baking dish and heat for 25 minutes.

JAM TARTS

**1 pack ready-made puff pastry (read the label to check for vegetable fat, not lard or suet)
1 jar of jam**

Turn the oven on to medium. Roll out the pastry as per instructions on the wrapper. Use the top of the jam jar as a pastry cutter and pop the circles into a greased tart tray. Fill with jam and bake 10 minutes. You'll burn your mouth if you don't let the jam cool down before eating.

TRIFLE

Don't let the title fool you. This is a very important recipe.

**1 bottle of sherry
1 box trifle mix
1 pint milk**

Drink all but 2 tablespoons of the sherry. Pour the remainder over the little sponge fingers and then follow the instructions on the box. By the time you've slept off the sherry, the trifle should be ready to eat!

A BOWL OF HEAVEN

1 banana
1 pack coffee Angel Delight
1 pack chocolate Angel Delight
1 pint milk
chocolate flake

Slice the banana and lay it on the bottom of a bowl. Mix up the coffee Angel Delight and pour into the bowl. Do the same with chocolate Angel Delight and pour on top. You don't need to wash the mixing bowl between times. Decorate with chocolate flake.

HALVA SANDWICH

Next time you visit a specialist emporium, buy a packet of this delightful 'cake' made with sesame seeds, sugar and vanilla. It's ideal to eat on its own or sliced thinly and laid between two thin slices of buttered bread.

CHOCOLATE SANDWICHES

1 packet butter biscuits
1 tub chocolate hazelnut spread

Spread a biscuit with the sticky stuff, drop another on top and shove into the orifice directly below the entrance to your respiratory system.

9

FRESH OFF THE TREE

JUNK FOOD SALADS

I am personally of the opinion that salads are not as healthy as we have been led to believe. Below are some of the most likely health hazards associated with raw vegetables, and tips on how to avoid them . . .

THE LINK BETWEEN SALADS AND PNEUMONIA . . .

If you've ever tried to prepare a salad in winter, you'll know all about this. Running each item in turn under a stream of icy water is enough to destroy the extremeties of the healthiest Vegetarian. I have experimented with warm water and can report that while my tiny hand was no longer frozen, my lettuce went decidedly limp. The ideal solution would seem to be rubber gloves. While not as tasty as many vegetables, they require far less preparation and their inedibility is a natural boon for those on a diet.

CARROT GRATER'S ELBOW . . .

There are three excellent ways to avoid this painful condition. The first is to eat your carrots whole. The second is to use an electric grater. The third is to buy your carrots ready grated from superior supermarkets. Failing this, you must treat the whole thing as physical exercise. Grip the carrot firmly in your right hand and hold the grater with your left. Make 10 positive downward strokes and then change hands! Once you've mastered this, you're ready for the hard bit. Lie down on the floor. Remove your shoes and socks. Grip the carrot in your left foot between the big toe and the first little stubby one. Support the grater with your right foot. After 10 strokes repeat the operation with the feet reversed. If you seriously wish to follow these instructions, you may wish to consult a chiropodist (or psychiatrist)!

TOMATO SLICER'S FINGER . . .

Nothing decorates a plate so well as a few thin slices of fresh tomato. For some people, this has become a dangerous obsession. By selecting an under-ripe tomato and a very sharp knife, it is possible to increase the number of thin slices obtainable. Any green on the tomato skin is disguised by blood released from the fingers via the sharp knife. This practice seems hardly suitable for Vegetarians. You may prefer to serve your tomatoes whole. Alternatively, when slicing, you should bear in mind the following point: *tomatoes* are (usually) round and red (or green), while *fingers* are (usually) sausage shaped and pink (or brown).

YOUR BASIC TOSSED GREEN

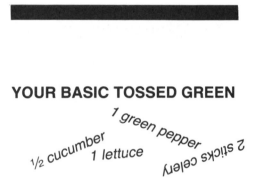

1 Strip off the outer leaves of the lettuce and throw them away. They are too much trouble. Get down to the heart and give it a quick inspection to make sure no dirt is trapped in it. Run it quickly under the cold tap and shake it out of the window. Grab a sharp knife and slice the whole thing like a loaf of bread. You should end up with shredded lettuce.

2 If you really *must* peel the cucumber, you've only yourself to blame for being fussy. I eat the skin 'cos its easier. It's also quicker to chop lengthways and then into chunks.

3 Give the 2 sticks of celery a quick rinse and wipe. Lay one on top of the other and slice them thinly together.

4 Rinse the pepper and slice into rings. Quarter each ring and discard seeds.

5 Mix the whole lot together and drown in the dressing of your choice.

YOUR BASIC CHUNKY RED

8 oz tomatoes
1 red pepper
1 small can sweetcorn
½ small red cabbage
1 bottle of sliced beetroot, drained

Wash and quarter the tomatoes. Rinse, ring, seed and quarter the pepper. Drain the sweetcorn. With a sharp knife slice the cabbage as thin as you can be bothered. Mix the whole lot together in a big bowl and then go and wash the beetroot off your hands! Serve with Slimmers Salad Cream because it doesn't contain eggs.

YOUR BASIC ARTY FARTY

4 oz frozen peas
½ Chinese leaf or small white cabbage
2 sticks celery
2 oz mixed nuts
1 box of cress
cottage cheese

Put the peas in a bowl and pour boiling water on them. Thinly slice the Chinese leaf or cabbage and celery. Mix with nuts and cress. The peas should now be defrosted. Rinse them in cold water to cool them down and sling them in the salad. Serve with cottage cheese.

(BASIC = Boring Awful Salads - Ingeniously Camouflaged!)

YOUR BASIC EXOTIC

1 head of chicory
1 ripe avocado
1 can Jerusalem artichokes, drained
4 oz alfalfa sprouts
oil and vinegar

Thinly slice the chicory. Quarter the avocado, scoop out the flesh and chop into chunks. Lay everything on a bed of alfalfa sprouts. Serve with oil and vinegar.

YOUR BASIC SWEET

1 large carrot
4 oz mixed nuts and raisins
½ red pepper, diced
1 crisp apple
lemon juice

Grate the carrot. Mix with the nuts and raisins and diced pepper. Just before serving, slice the apple into chunks (don't peel it) and squirt lemon juice everywhere to stop it going brown.

SIMPLE DRESSING

As a general rule, there are so many dressings on the shelves of your shop that you should never need to make one. However, the simplest recipe is . . .

1 tablespoon oil (any old vegetable oil will do)
1 tablespoon malt vinegar
1 good squeeze lemon juice
1 teaspoon soy sauce

Put all ingredients in an empty bottle and shake well.

TOFU SALAD

If you used to like egg salad, you'll love this. Tofu is a sort of 'soya' cheese that you buy fresh, in pieces from a Chinese supermarket.

3 pieces Chinese tofu
1 cup eggless salad cream
¼ raw onion, finely chopped
1 teaspoon turmeric
chopped parsley
lemon juice⎫
paprika ⎬ to sprinkle on top

The tofu looks a little weird and wonderful. Slice it into little cubes (about ¼ inch) and pop it in a mixing bowl. Add everything else and give it a really good stir. Squeeze some lemon juice and shake some paprika over the top. This also goes well in sandwiches.

COLESLAW

You can buy this ready made, but it tends to be swimming in eggy mayonnaise. Some people are lucky enough to live near supermarkets that sell ready-grated cabbage and carrot. If you don't, and you like coleslaw, invest in an electric grater.

8 oz carrots
½ small white cabbage
eggless salad cream

Grate the carrots, thinly slice the cabbage, mix and add salad cream. The longer you leave it, the soggier it gets!
  N.B. you can also try adding all or any of the following . . .

2 oz mixed nuts
2 oz sultanas
¼ chopped onion
4 oz grated cheese

MAGIC TOMATOES

This will look as if it took you ages but it's dead quick.

8 firm tomatoes
8 oz cottage cheese
1 small bag salted roast almonds

Slice off the top of the tomatoes. Scoop out half the middle and throw it away (or get someone to show you how to make coronets). Stuff till overflowing with cottage cheese and top with almonds.

GUACAMOLE

For this you need *ripe* avocados. They should at least rattle when you shake them, or better still be squishy to the touch.

2 ripe avocados
eggless salad cream
chilli powder, salt, pepper, chopped parsley
a few pieces of chopped onion (definitely optional)
1 clove garlic, finely chopped (see onions)

Slice the avocados in half and remove the stone. In theory you can plant this, but I can never work out which end to put in the soil! Scoop out the flesh and mash with 2 hefty shakes of salad cream and everything else. Shove it in sandwiches, serve it with chips, sling it on salads, try it with tortilla chips . . .

Theory A

Whatever the habit you're trying to beat, constant nibbling can often help. Cut out cigarettes, alcohol and lovers but nibble on these with impunity.

Theory B

Constant eating makes you fat. Don't eat these, have more sex, booze and fags instead.

YOGHURT DIP

1 good pinch cinnamon
1 carton plain yoghurt
2 tablespoons thick honey
2 crisp apples
lemon or lime juice

Mix the cinnamon and yoghurt and pop in a bowl. Put the honey in another bowl. Slice the apple into thin wedges and squeeze lemon or lime juice over it to stop it going brown. Dip the apple first in honey, then in yoghurt.

DIP STICKS

2 large courgettes
2 large carrots
4 sticks of celery
4 oz cottage cheese

Slice the vegetables lengthways into thin sticks. Dip in the cheese.

or use them whole — in which case — this recipe becomes the "BIG DIPPER"(!

SKINNY DIPS

Make potato skins (see p. 30). Serve with guacamole (see p. 61) or sour cream.

LUCKY DIPS

4 oz raw broccoli
oil and vinegar dressing

Dip the heads of broccoli in the dressing and munch. Eat as much (or little) of the stalk as you fancy!

ROAD DIPS AHEAD

Going on a long journey? I am reliably informed that there are still one or two remote parts of the universe where the long-distance traveller cannot be guaranteed a Vegetarian repast at any hour of the day or night. Should you ever find yourself in this situation, make up some of this . . .

fresh chopped thyme
4 oz grated Cheddar cheese
4 oz cottage cheese
a few pieces of finely chopped onion
salt and pepper
8 oz baby raw carrots

Mix the thyme (who knows where it goes?) with the cheeses and onion. Add a spot of salt and pepper.

Now here's the clever part. Put it all in one of those plastic tubs with a lid. Carry the carrots in a plastic bag in your other pocket. Use the carrots as a sort of clumsy, messy and ever-diminishing spoon!

RAITTA

Traditionally served as an accompaniment to curry, this cooling concoction goes just as well with any hot and spicy dish. (The above sentence was loaned by kind permission of the Delia Craddock school of normal cookery book writing.)

½ small cucumber
1 tub plain yoghurt
pinch of salt, pepper
small squirt lemon juice
paprika

Peel and dice the cucumber. Mix it with the yoghurt, salt, pepper and lemon juice. Sprinkle paprika on top and keep chilled till needed.

ONION RAITTA: As above but with a few *thin* slices of onion mixed in as well.

TOMATO RAITTA: As Onion Raitta but with chopped tomato too.

PAPERBACK RAITTA: There's no such thing but I couldn't resist the joke.

10

THE MAN WHO LIVED ON BREAD AND CHEESE

A SANDWICH SAGA

What you are about to read is completely true. Only the names have been changed to protect the innocent.

It is North London, during an endless summer. High above the city, in an untidy bedsit, our hero – a handsome bronzed writer – is hard at work on his latest bestseller. Night after night he hunches over his word processor with only the clack of the keys and his jazz piano records for company.

The relentless pressure of publisher's deadlines are upon him. What little spare time he has is spent fighting off the advances of thousands of beautiful women who flock to his door.

Ironically, for he is writing a book on food, it seems there is little time to cook. Only an endless supply of bread and cheese from the corner delicatessen keeps him from starvation.

The following excerpts from his diary are reprinted exactly as they appear . . . *(... well almost !)*

THE MAN WHO LIVED ON BREAD AND CHEESE...

MONDAY 4am: The relentless pressure of publisher's deadlines is upon me.It's hard being a handsome bronzed writer with only the clack of my word processor and jazz piano records for company.This weekend I've eaten rye bread and Gouda, muffins and cream cheese, crumpets and Cheshire, croissants and Brie, bagels and Cheddar. I can't wait for tomorrow when the shops open. I shall leap out and buy teacakes and cottage cheese or perhaps pitta bread and fetta. Can't write anymore tonight. More beautiful women are ringing my doorbell...

CHEESE ON TOAST

Even people who swear blind that they can't cook have no trouble making this dish. Like walking, speaking and complaining about the weather, the ability to make cheese on toast is a natural human function and separates us from the rest of the animal kingdom. We all have our preferences for different sorts of cheese and different sorts of bread and the technique of grilling them together hardly needs explanation. Vegetarians, however, eat considerably more of this dish than carnivores – and consequently have a greater need for variety within it. This is where my experience as a master chef may be of use to you! The real fun is in shoving things on top of or underneath the cheese. Rather like empty washing up liquid bottles, the things you can do with cheese on toast are limited only by the imagination.

ON TOP OF THE CHEESE . . . try adding all or any of the following: *sliced* mushrooms, onions, green peppers, tomatoes, vegetarian frankfurters.

BELOW THE CHEESE . . . try adding all or any of the following: *sliced* beetroot, avocado, cucumber, banana, pineapple, apple, pre-cooked potatoes, nutmeat, etc.

* Although this dish is fundamental to carnivores and Vegetarians alike, I've never seen two people cook it the same way. Perhaps it's the very simplicity of the concept that demands such individualistic, creative self expression. Or perhaps it is the implied sexual symbolism inherent in the process. Under the heat of passion (represented by the grill), the cheese (female or yin) softens and expands to completely envelope the bread (male or yang), which stiffens in response. Thus the infinite variations to be found in the making of cheese and toast echo and reflect the infinite variations of attitude to be found in the act of lovemaking itself. The pioneering psychologist, Carl Jung, coined the terms *Anima* and *Animus* to explain our widely differing and highly personal reactions to erotic stimuli. It is not beyond the bounds of credibility to suggest that he obviously developed these theories while engaged in the highly symbolic act of preparing a Welsh Rarebit.

Also BELOW THE CHEESE, you could spread a small dollop of: peanut butter, marmite, canned macaroni cheese, mushy peas, left-over curry, left-over stew, etc. *Note*: with all these things, it's advisable to grill them on their own for a few moments before adding the cheese. See example below.

CHEESE AND BEANS ON TOAST

4 slices of bread
butter
1 small can baked beans
several slices of cheese

Grill one side of the bread. Butter the soft side and lay on a hefty spoonful of baked beans. Grill for 2 minutes. Cover with the cheese and grill again till the cheese melts.
  No washing up!

The best way to slice cheese is with a medieval torture instrument that you buy from posh department stores – a stainless steel roller with a piece of wire stretched tightly across the top giving nice thin slices. Avoid graters at all costs. They are a pain to clean and take too much effort.

PITTA BREAD

Gives a high surface area and low bulk. It allows you to concentrate on toppings. Warm the pitta under the grill for a few moments, turning it once. it should puff up slightly. Insert a sharp knife, as if you were going to open up the pocket, but actually *separate* the two halves.

CHEESE AND TOMATO PITTA

1 pitta bread, halved (see above)
butter
4 oz tomatoes
oregano, salt, pepper
plenty of sliced Edam cheese
cress

Butter the pitta halves. Slice the tomatoes thinly and lay on top. Shove under the grill for 2 minutes. Pull out and sprinkle on seasoning. Cover with cheese (leave no gaps) and bung back under the grill till the cheese is all bubbly and runny. Garnish with cress, and use a paper serviette to hold it.

CHEESE, TOMATO AND MUSHROOM PITTA: Make the above, but after the cheese has begun to melt, add 4 oz thinly-sliced fresh mushrooms and re-grill for a further 2 minutes.

CHEESE, TOMATO, MUSHROOM AND ONION PITTA: As above, but when the mushrooms begin to shrink, add another layer of cheese and top with *thinly*-sliced raw onions. Re-grill for 2 minutes.

You can carry on like this till you run out of ideas.

THE ABOVE RECIPES . . .

can of course be made with other sorts of bread. Here's a tip. Only toast ONE side of the bread. Put the topping on the soft side. It will stop you getting burnt edges.

Here is by far the best way to make pizza appear on your table.

Look in the Yellow Pages.

Phone up a Pizza house.

Place your order.

Go and fetch it.

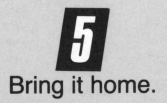

Bring it home.

NEO PIZZA

This recipe calls for a generous tablespoon. To find out if it's really generous, ask it to lend you a fiver!

1 can or bottle spaghetti sauce
1 pitta bread
2 oz fresh mushrooms, sliced
Mozzarella cheese
oregano
olives, stoned

Spread a generous tablespoon of sauce on each pitta half. Top with thinly-sliced mushrooms and grill for 2 minutes. Cover in thin slices of Mozzarella. (Cheats can use Edam or Gouda.)
   Grill again, and just before serving add a pinch of oregano and stoned olives. (To check if they're properly stoned, hold the jar to your ear. You should hear words like 'far out, man' and 'wow' above the noise of old Grateful Dead records.)

WEDNESDAY 5.43am... The endless clack of the word processor keys is beginning to get on my nerves. The collection of jazz records is wearing thin. Only the endless procession of beautiful women keeps me from despair. Never mind. I've finished the section on sandwiches at last. Here it is.

SANDWICHES

For a Vegetarian, the word 'sandwich' brings to mind a plethora of delicious alternative fillings. There's cheese, cheese, cheese, cheese, cheese and (just for a change) cheese*. It can be *so* hard to make a choice! Seriously though, if you are fond of sandwiches but cheesed off with you-know-what, the best thing to do is experiment. There are surprisingly few things that can't be squeezed between two slices of bread successfully – and these include many of the TVP products mentioned in Chapter 7. Varying the sort of bread you use can help too. Finally, the intelligent reader will not need to be told that in addition to the following list, almost all the suggestions for 'Cheese on Toast' can be used cold in sandwiches.

I hope you haven't been brainwashed by the 'brown is beautiful' brigade. Wholemeal bread is too stiff to make a decent sandwich. You can't cram enough ingredients in.

Always butter both sides. If in doubt, add salt and pepper. Don't be afraid to experiment. If you're making them to eat later, wrap them in clingfilm and keep 'em cool.

Most sandwiches perk up considerably with a shake of salt and pepper and some finely chopped parsley.

POTATOES . . . are, of course, cooked canned potatoes, sliced into thin pieces.

AVOCADOS . . . Should be ripe. ⅓ is enough for one sandwich – more than that and you'll need to wear a bib and eat it in private. Very squishy ones should be mashed onto the bread. Otherwise, lay on thick slices. Always add salt and pepper.

---

* CATHARSIS CORNER
The whole business of cheese is made even harder if you're strict about the kind of cheese you eat. Technically, a lot of commercial cheese contains small quantities of rennet to make it set. Rennet is normally made from the lining of a calf's stomach. Only certain sorts of Dutch, soft and 'special vegetarian' cheese are exempt. I do try and stick to these when I can, but it's not always easy. For this reason, I've not specified the kind of cheese in many recipes. That way, each one of us can indulge in a private battle between tastebuds and conscience.

MARMITE . . . Should be spread thinly.

TARTEX . . . Is a pâté made from yeast. It comes in cans or tubes from health stores.

ALFALFA SPROUTS . . . Add a jolly crunch. They come from health shops and enlightened supermarkets. No washing is required. Just pop a LARGE handful in the sandwich with some salt.

MISO . . . Is a weird-looking paste that you either love or hate. A sort of solid soy sauce, it comes in expensive packets from health stores.

SAUSALATAS AND NUT LOAF . . . Come in cans from health stores. Use plenty!

UNUSUAL COMBINATIONS

Cheese, pickle and alfalfa
Cheese & tortilla chips
Cheese & marmalade (try it)
Cheese & green pepper
Cheese, onion & Sausalata
Cheese & cold baked beans
Cottage cheese & raw
  mushroom
Cottage cheese & fried
  mushrooms
Cottage cheese & avocado
Creamcheese & canned
  sweetcorn

Creamcheese & celery
Creamcheese, beansprouts
  & beetroot
Creamcheese, avocado &
  alfalfa
Smoked cheese & lettuce
  heart
Guacamole & lettuce
Tofu salad & tomato
Cucumber
Cucumber, potato & miso
Miso & peanut butter
Nutloaf & mushroom

Potato + marmite

Avocado, cheese, raw mushrooms + alfalfa...

Marmite, peanut butter, cream cheese + Jam !!

Tortex + Tomato

Avocado + chicory (add plenty of salt + pepper)

cream cheese + canned

72

11

Not so long ago, fruit juice was unheard of in many countries. Shops were crammed to overflowing with squashes, cordials and barley waters. Beer, wine, milk and Coca Cola flowed like water but FRUIT JUICE? You might as well have walked into your local store and asked for video cassettes or computer software!

Fruit juice is brimming with Vitamin C and Junk Food Vegetarians will need little encouragement to take full advantage. Below, for your edification, enlightenment and enjoyment . . .

USES FOR JUICES

THE LIQUID DIET

MANGO JUICE

This subtle combination of refreshing liquid from Asia and Russia was invented one Christmas in Leeds. We called it an 'Eastern Bloc'.

1 litre mango juice
½ litre tonic water
1 bottle of vodka

Mix all ingredients in a large bucket with ice. Sip through a straw! It is not advisable to drive after drinking this, but you may wish to push your friends home in a supermarket trolley.

APPLE JUICE

This recipe calls for apple concentrate. You can buy it in a (cough) health store.

1 big bottle white vodka
1 litre Perrier water
1 bottle apple juice concentrate

1 part vodka, 1 part Perrier, 3 parts apple concentrate. If you can't get apple concentrate, use ordinary apple juice and tell it to pay attention!

PINEAPPLE JUICE

You need a blender to make this properly. Otherwise, there'll be a whole lot of shakin' going on.

1 tub coconut cream (health store again)
3 litres pineapple juice
1 big bottle white rum
ice

You won't, of course, get all this in the blender at once. The proportions are equal thirds of everything. Use plenty of ice, which, when blended, should make it thick like a milk shake.

GRAPEFRUIT JUICE

Those with 'sophisticated' tastes will appreciate the subtle tang of this delicate concoction. Those without sophisticated tastes won't care after the second glass.

1 litre grapefruit juice
1 half bottle gin
1 litre bitter lemon

1 lime

Mix 2 parts grapefruit juice to 1 part gin. Add loads of ice, bitter lemon to taste, and decorate with slices of lime.

Using a slide rule, or a small computer, or a team of mathematicians working round the clock, it should be possible to reduce these quantities in a ratio suitable for smaller servings.

ORANGE JUICE (1)

Squeezing oranges can be a sensual experience. Drinking fresh squeezed juice *is* a sensual experience. Sharing this recipe with the right person may lead to a *very* sensual experience.

1 bottle white rum
1 bottle of Galliano
Oceans of fresh squeezed orange juice

2 parts rum, 1 part Galliano, 3 part O.J. Shake the whole lot together and pour over ice.

ORANGE JUICE (2)

Tequila includes an extract of the cactus from which mescaline is made. Tequila includes an extract of the cactus from which mescaline is made. It gives some people double vision.

1 bottle tequila
1 bottle grenadine
2 litres orange juice

Pour a shot of tequila into a glass. Pop a dash of grenadine in it. Top with orange juice. I call this a Tequila Sunset because, if you don't stir it, it has layers of golden colour.

What's the difference between a Tequila Sunset and Tequila Sunrise? . . . About 9 hours!

TOMATO JUICE

Alcohol, they say, depletes the body's reserve of Vitamin C. Tomato juice puts it back! Surely this is Yin and Yang at their most complementary. The essential duality of the universe encapsulated in an elementary balance between ... *zzzzzz* !

3 parts tomato juice
1 part vodka
dash of soy sauce

This drink is not quite a Bloody Mary because a Bloody Mary contains Worcestershire Sauce. Worcestershire Sauce contains anchovies. Anchovies are little dead fishes. This is a Bloodless Mary.

GRAPE JUICE

Whether or not it is alcoholic, grape juice is usually better drunk straight. This recipe is an exception to that advice and it's great for winter parties.

3 litres cheap red wine
1 tablespoon cinnamon
1 teaspoon mixed spice
6 oz brown sugar
apples and lemons, sliced

Put everything in a big saucepan over a low heat and stir. Let it get hot, but *don't* let it boil. Decorate with thin slices of apple and lemon. Pour into mugs.

It is just possible, after drinking all or any of the aforementioned, that you may feel in need of a little pick-me-up. By far the best cure is the 'hair of the dog', but you'll also find the following non-alcoholic drinks helpful.

CHAI

This delightful beverage comes from the foothills of the Himalayas. The recipe was given to me by a wandering yogi(ess) called Teresa.

1 cup of milk
1 cup of water
2 cardamom pods
1 dash of mixed spice
1 teabag
brown sugar or honey to taste

Optional extras:
a little bit of nutmeg
a cinnamon stick
a little ginger root
a tiny piece of ginseng root

Bring the milk, water and spices to the boil. Add the teabag and simmer the lot for a few minutes. Sweeten to taste and sip slowly chanting *Om Mani padne om*. (Himalayan for 'What time is the next bus to Dehra Dun?')

MOCHA COFFEE

1 sachet instant hot chocolate mix
whipped cream

Make up with coffee, not boiling water. Top with instant whipped cream.

12

ICKY DIDDUMS COOCHY DEN

FEEDING THE NEXT GENERATION

Children are different to grown-ups. For one thing, they're shorter. For another, they're a lot more sensitive. It's amazing how many Vegetarian parents get cold feet when it comes to feeding their kids. They believe all that rubbish about eggs, fish and meat being good for growing bodies.

I can't be flippant about children's nutrition. They *shouldn't* be encouraged to live on bubble gum and Coca Cola. At the same time, they needn't be force-fed brown rice and cabbage and they certainly *don't* need dead bodies or their embryos to make them healthy.

Protein is important but a regular intake of bread, cheese, milk and baked beans will take care of all their needs in that direction. Remember, Vitamin C is in home-made chips as well as oranges. Vitamins A, B complex, D and E are all in milk, cheese and butter. If they turn up their noses at your carefully made salads and groan at boiled cabbage, don't worry. Give them beans, chips and soya sausages. Relax. They're getting what they need.

If you let them indulge in puddings and pizzas, you won't be doing them too much harm as long as the spoonful of sugar contains *some* medicine, and you watch the rest of their diet. Better that they clean their teeth than develop a complex about forbidden food.

Happy, loved and un-hassled kids instinctively eat well. Fret, fuss or nag at them and they'll just make an issue out of it and lose their natural discretion.

Here endeth the lecture.

Kids don't seem to have the same need for variety that adults do. They like to stick with their favourite things. They also prefer blander tastes and really respond to food that is well presented or decorated. Here are some 'fun' recipes.

COW PIE
(serves 2-4)

Just like Desperate Dan's Auntie used to serve.
You can buy pie crust ready made from most supermarkets, or use thawed frozen pastry (the
brands without lard).

½ SMALL PACK SOSMIX
1 CAN POTATOES
1 READY-MADE PIE CRUST
2 SMALL WASHED CARROTS
1 LONG CARROT

Put the oven on medium. Make up some Sosmix
and open a can of potatoes. Mix the Sosmix
and potatoes together and fill the pie. Shove
the fat ends of two small carrots into one
side to make horns. You can use various
things to make the tail. An asparagus tip,
a suitable strand of parsley or just half a
long carrot sliced lengthways. Bake for
20 minutes.

SPACE INVADERS SPECIAL
(serves 2)

4 OZ MILK
4 SLICES OF WHITE BREAD
1 CAN HEINZ SPACE INVADERS
VEGETABLE OIL
6 BUTTON MUSHROOMS
1 CARTON COTTAGE CHEESE

1. Pour the milk in a shallow tray. Cut the slices of bread in half and soak them in the milk for 5 minutes.

2. Heat up the Space Invaders.

3. Put some oil in a frying pan and, when it is hot, drop in the bread. It will sizzle something rotten. Shake the pan a little and, after about a minute, turn over the bread and do the other side.

4. Drop the mushrooms in whole and let them fry for a minute or two.

5. Arrange each plate with four slices of fried bread as a frame. Spread a layer of cottage cheese inside the lower third of the frame. Fill the top two-thirds with invaders. Pop the three mushrooms on top of the cottage cheese.

BANGERS AND MASH

(serves 2)

2 CANS BOILED POTATOES
6 VEGETARIAN SAUSAGES
BUTTER
MILK
SALT.

Make up the mash as on p. 18. Make it quite stiff and heap it in a big mountain on the plate. Heat the sausages and poke them into it so that the ends stick out.

Just like in the cartoons.

BOATS

(Serves 2 hungry kids)

2 LARGE BAKED POTATOES
1 SMALL CAN BAKED BEANS
2 CRISP LETTUCE LEAVES
2 THIN DRINKING STRAWS
BLUE FOOD DYE

Hollow out the baked potatoes, leaving about ½ inch of flesh. These are your boats. Take out the remainder of the flesh and mix with one or two drops of blue food dye. This is your sea. Cover each plate with a thin layer of sea. Fill the boats with cooked baked beans. Take your lettuce leaves, which should be white and crisp (from the heart). These are your sails. The drinking straws are masts. Spear each leaf through a straw and bung in the middle of each boat.

Serve with a smile and (depending on the age of the kids) a stern warning NOT to eat the straws.

13

LEND US A FIVER TILL FRIDAY

There comes a time in most people's lives when the electricity bill arrives on the same day as the phone bill in the week that your car is being serviced and your two best friends are having birthdays.

These occasions may demand economy in the wealthiest of income brackets and the following tips are worth remembering.

BARGAINS

As a general rule, you get best value for money at a greengrocers. If you're strapped for cash, avoid health stores like the plague and lay off the canned and frozen food.

Your best bets are spuds and curry powder. Potatoes are cheap and versatile. You can also make almost anything into a curry of sorts. Chop whatever you have handy into small chunks. Fry it up in oil, starting with the hardest items and ending with the softest. Hurl in plenty of curry powder, water and a tin of tomatoes. The longer you simmer it, the better it tastes (up to a maximum of 20 minutes).

Supermarkets often mark down dairy produce and veg that's reached its sell-by date. Late Friday nights, Saturday afternoons and early Monday mornings are good times to find these.

FREEBIES

Dandelion leaves can be picked and cooked like spinach.

At certain times of the year, you can gather wild mushrooms in the local park. If you go there, you'll probably notice some wide eyed, laughing young people doing the same thing. Explain that you want the *non* psychedelic variety and chances are they'll be able to point them out for you. (You may find a more reliable source of this information in the local library.)

If you're really penniless, remember that *fasting* sounds a lot groovier than *starving*. It won't do you any harm to eat no food at all for a day or two. (Drink plenty of water though.) You'll also end up high as a kite, which is why it's such a popular activity amongst the quasi-spiritual. Break your fast *gently* . . . your stomach will have shrunk a little.

A LESS DRASTIC SOLUTION

When you buy processed food, you're paying someone else to prepare it. You may well feel that your time is too valuable to waste at the stove. Even if you're broke, borrow a fiver, buy something quick and turn the time to something more profitable.

14

WE WISH YOU A MERRY....

It's Christmas Eve in the TV studio and the set is draped in wilting tinsel. The presenter, who is nearly as bored as the viewing audience, smiles stupidly into the autocue and reads:

'Tomorrow, most people are looking forward to a nice fat roast turkey with all the trimmings. Tonight, let's spare a thought for the thousands of British Vegetarians who will be deprived of this wonderful treat. In the studio tonight we have Dorothy Buckwheat, author of *Know Your Onions* and *2000 Ways with Lentils*. Dorothy, what will YOU be having for Christmas Dinner?'

'Well, every Christmas, our family sits down to a delicious meal of roasted peanuts and lettuce. We wash it down with Holdenbergs 200 per cent pure imported turnip juice.'

'Gosh, that's fascinating, Dotty. What about Christmas Pudding?'

'Oh, we don't miss out on that . . . I make a special sugar-free version with bran and organic prunes.'

'Great. Well, thank you very much for coming along tonight, Dotty.' (Turns to camera and smiles) 'Meanwhile for those of us with less healthy inclinations, here is Sarah Butcherson with an interesting way to stuff your turkey . . .'

It is true that a lot of traditional Christmas fare is not Vegetarian. Turkeys are innocent birds. They are kept in tiny cages, overfed and then strangled to save bullets. Mincemeat oozes suet. Suet is made from pigfat.

Here's a complete Christmas menu. You won't make it in 10 minutes, but you will find it a very acceptable alternative to death on a plate.

TURKEY

1 13-oz pack Sosmix

Make up Sosmix as on pack. Leave it to set.

STUFFING

1 packet Burgamix
1 small onion
handful of fresh or dried sage
1 large grated carrot

1 Make up ¼ of the Burgamix. Finely chop the onion and mix with ALL other ingredients. Leave it to set and then roll into a big fat sausage.

2 Take a large baking tray and smear it generously with butter or margarine. Grab about one-third of the Sosmix and roll it out into a flat pancake. Use a little flour on the rolling pin to stop it sticking and more on the table top for the same reason.

3 Lay your Sosmix pancake on the baking tray and pop the stuffing on top. Cover the stuffing with two-thirds of the remaining Sosmix so that you have a circular pink mountain. To join the Sosmix top to the Sosmix bottom, you may need to use a little water.

4 Shape the remaining Sosmix into wings and attach one to each side of the turkey. (The first time I made this, I added a head with currants for the eyes, but I was told that meat eaters don't like this!)

5 Pop it on the middle shelf of the oven and turn the oven on to medium. Take out 45 minutes later.

ROAST POTATOES

See p. 17.

BRUSSELS SPROUTS

1 lb frozen Brussels sprouts

Drop in a pan containing half an inch of salted boiling water, cover and simmer for 5 minutes.

MUSHROOMS AND ONIONS

8 oz frozen baby onions
butter
1 lb fresh button mushrooms

Fry the baby onions in butter for about 2 minutes. Add the whole, rinsed mushrooms and cover. Sizzle on a low heat for 5 minutes.

APPLE SAUCE

Buy a bottle of apple sauce!

VEGETABLE SAUCE

4 oz fresh sliced mushrooms
½ pint milk
1 packet golden vegetable soup
salt and pepper

Fry the mushrooms, pour on the milk, stir in the soup-mix and cook till thick. Add salt and pepper, transfer into a jug and keep warm till ready to serve.

CHRISTMAS SALAD

1 stick celery
3 large carrots, grated
8 oz vegetarian cheese, grated
4 oz mixed nuts
2 oz raisins
a tiny pinch of nutmeg

Garnish:
cress
cottage cheese
tomato

Finely chop the stick of celery, then mix all the ingredients together. Garnish with cress, cottage cheese and thinly sliced tomato.

MINCE PIES

Shop-bought mince pies are loaded with suet and lard. Go to a health store and buy a jar of vegetarian mincemeat. Make up your own pastry, or buy some *non* lardy, frozen puff pastry.

Home-made ones taste much nicer.

CHRISTMAS PUDDING

Once again, I have to admit that the health store is the place to go. You can buy suet-free puddings and they're really good. Cover the 5p pieces with silver foil before you stick them in.

CHRISTMAS CAKE

It IS possible to make cake without eggs, but you've got to be a good cook. The following recipe is courtesy of my ex-wife, who though inspiring this book with her love of brown rice, could make a hell of a cake if you managed to jog her elbow while she was pouring in the sugar. It is *not* a Junk Food Vegetarian recipe but – what the hell . . . it's Christmas!

10 oz butter
10 oz soft brown sugar
1 lb self raising flour
1 orange
1 lemon
6 oz sultanas
6 oz raisins
1 banana, mashed
4 oz ground almonds
1 teaspoon cinnamon
1 teaspoon mixed spice
¼ cup sherry
1 teaspoon vinegar
1 tablespoon milk

Leave the butter in a dish above the fire till it's very soft. Mix with the sugar and the flour. (It's worth borrowing a mixer.)

Grate the orange and lemon peel and drop it in. Mixed dried peel tastes revolting as far as I'm concerned but you could use that if you want, instead. Juice the fruit and pour that in too.

Ideally, you should wind up with a mixture that is quite runny. Just shove in all the other ingredients and keep mixing, adding milk where necessary to keep it runny. If you end up with something ridiculously too wet, pour in a bit more flour. Following these principles, you needn't really weigh the ingredients, but simply guess, adding or deleting the things you like or hate!

Preheat the oven to 300°F/Gas 2. (i.e. turn it on at that level and leave it for about 10 minutes.)

Get 1 big or 2 small cake tins and GREASE them well with butter and your fingers. Dump in the cake mixture and pop it on the middle shelf for 1½ hours. Turn out and leave to cool.

Buy some marzipan, roll it out and cover the cake.

ICING

1 lb icing sugar
8 oz soft butter
1 teaspoon vanilla

Mix together all ingredients, possibly adding a little water if it is too stiff. Lavish generously on top of the marzipan.

CHRISTMAS DRINKS

It may not be traditional, but champagne or sparkling wine is lovely with all the above.

15
ONE STOP SHOPPING

HOW TO FIND WHAT YOU WANT
WHERE YOU WANT

Almost everything you need to be a Junk Food Vegetarian can be bought from a supermarket.* In the recipe sections, I've tried to stick to the kind of things that are common to most retailers. Remember though, that no two chain stores are ever the same. Learn to shop around and get into the habit of *READING LABELS*.

If you're conscientious about avoiding meat, the words to avoid are: animal fats, shortening, beef extract, gelatine (crushed bones). This rules out many brands of biscuits, cakes and packet soups.** Quite a few manufacturers have recently stopped putting slaughterhouse by-products into things, so by joining the boycott you can help persuade the rest.

It's often surprising what you can find that is 'kosher' for vegetarians! If you live near an ethnic store, or one of the up-market supermarket chains, you'll find a cornucopia of luxuries that have never seen a dead body in their lives.

Most shopkeepers are only too pleased to answer questions such as 'What is it?' and 'What's in it?' They tend not to respond so well to, 'What does it taste like?' (Which is, if you think about it, a silly question. Try it and see!)

Chinese stores sell Tofu (bean curd) and exotic vegetables.

Indian shops sell vegetable samosas, curried dhal (lentils), Pakra and popadoms.

Greek establishments have Halloumi and Feta (two incredible cheeses), tahini (try a spoonful in a sauce], halva, and vine leaves stuffed with rice. (Not to mention some amazing yoghurt.)

Jewish delicatessens have bagels, falafel, hummous, rye bread, borscht, latkes, etc.

Up-market supermarkets often sell these things too, and you can often find ready-made vegetarian meals in their fridges or freezers.

---

* The exception is TVP (imitation meat). It is about the only useful thing you'll find in most health food shops.

** A lot of goodies (frozen cakes and fresh pasta) contain eggs. I have been known to weaken under their charm occasionally!

In short then, you would do well to take a few leisurely trips round different shops. If you don't like shopping much, stock up on lots of things and you won't have to go back for a while.

WHY THIS INDEX IS NOT BORING!

Here, thanks to the wonder of the word processor, is a (hopefully) complete index of ingredients mentioned in this book. As you've no doubt sussed by now, the real art in being a fast food, Junk food, groovy Vegetarian is to keep well-stocked cupboards. To help you, I've arranged the index as a shopping list. The idea is that you can photocopy* it a few times and take it with you to the stores.

The ingredients are listed according to whether they come in cans, packs, frozen bags, bottles or whatever. The astute reader will notice that several items are repeated. That's because a lot of things can be found in fresh, frozen and canned forms. Although I've normally specified which form is best, generally speaking things are interchangeable in these recipes. (You'll soon find out the things that aren't!!!) With the exception of the 'Health Store' list, everything you see below should be obtainable from any large, posh, licensed supermarket.

The fresh stuff, of course, can also be found at your local green-grocer's – and I wouldn't stock up quite as much in that department for obvious reasons! (Mind you, most veggies will keep for up to a week in the bottom of your fridge.)

I've also included a few staples that you won't find mentioned in the book – but if you're going to have a shopping list, it might as well be useful. Well, that about wraps it up. I hope you found (at least some of) the jokes funny and (at least some of) the recipes edible. May the bluebird of happiness tweet merrily on your shoulder . . .

Jonathan Cainer

---

* This is technically illegal – but I won't tell if you don't!

IN THE SUPERMARKET

The things in CAPITAL LETTERS are 'staples'. Page numbers are not always given for these because they come up so much in the book!

STAPLE SECTION

BREAD (20, 67–72, 82)
   Burger buns (45)
   Hot dog rolls (41)
   Pitta bread (34, 46, 67–72)
Coffee
Jam (54)
Ketchup (41)
Lemon juice (38, 59, 60, 62, 64)
Liver salts
Marmalade (72)
Marmite (49, 70–72)
Mustard (41, 70–72)
Peanut butter (34, 70–72)
Pickle (70–72)
Pickled cucumbers
Pickled onions
Relish (46)
Salad cream (slimmers) (60, 61, 70–72)
Salt
Soap
Shampoo
Sugar (brown) (76, 77, 88)
Teabags (77)
Toilet roll
Toothpaste
Vegetable oil
Vinegar (38, 59, 63, 88)
Washing up liquid

CANNED STUFF

Artichoke hearts (59)
Asparagus (26)
Asparagus soup (26, 36)
Aubergines in sauce (28)
BAKED BEANS (43, 67–72, 83)
Bamboo shoots (31)
CANNED TOMATOES (24)
Celery soup (34, 38)
Chickpeas (35)
Curry cooking sauce (33, 47)
Custard (canned) (51, 52)
Golden veg soup (86)
Goulash cooking sauce (29)
Green beans (28, 42)
'Invaders' (80)
Kidney beans (30)
Macaroni cheese (24)
Mixed vegetables (29, 33, 38, 46)
MUSHROOMS
Mushroom soup (22)
POTATOES (cooked) (29, 38, 70–72, 79, 81)
Peach slices (53)
Peas (23, 25, 45, 47, 58)
Pineapple chunks (53)
Ratatouille (20, 21)
Rice (cooked) (18, 23, 33)
Spaghetti sauce (27, 68–69)
Spinach (25, 28, 48)
Spring veg soup (28, 44)
Strawberries (53)
Sweet & sour cooking sauce (32)
SWEETCORN (23, 24, 29, 48, 58, 70–72)
Taco sauce (30)
Tomato soup (49)

BOTTLED STUFF

Apple sauce (86)
Chilli peppers (34)
Honey (62)
Chocolate hazelnut spread
    (55)
Spaghetti sauce (27, 68–69)

DRIED & PACKET STUFF

Almonds (roast) (61)
Angel Delight: coffee &
    chocolate (55)
Biscuits* (51, 55)
Cheese sauce mix* (24)
Crisps
Fettucine (25)
Flour (self-raising) (88)
Goulash sauce mix* (29)
Hot chocolate mix (77)
Instant mashed potato
Lasagna (26)
Nuts (mixed) (58, 59, 60, 86)
Onions
Peanuts (dry roast) (38)
Raisins (38, 59, 86, 88)
RICE
Spaghetti (27)
Spaghetti sauce mix (27,
    68–69)
Sultanas (52, 54, 60, 88)
Sweet & sour mix (32)
TACO KITS (30)
Tagliatelle (25)
Tortilla chips (67–72)
SOUPS*
    Asparagus (26, 36)
    Celery (34, 38)
    Golden veg (86)
    Mushroom (22)
    Tomato (49)
    Spring veg (28, 44)

* Means check ingredients list on
pack: some silly manufacturers use
animal fats.

BAKING SECTION

Almonds (ground) (88)
Apple pie filling (51)
Blue food dye (82)
Chocolate flakes (55)
Chocolate sauce (52)
Custard (instant) (51, 52)
Icing sugar (89)
Marzipan (88)
Sponge cake mix (51)
Trifle mix (54)
Vanilla (89)
Wafers (52)

SPICE RACK

Black pepper
Cardamom pods (77)
Chilli powder (61)
Cinnamon (53, 54, 62, 76, 88)
Garlic (22, 25, 36, 38, 41, 61)
Nutmeg (54, 77, 86)
Mixed herbs (24, 25)
Mixed spice (76, 77, 88)
Oregano (22, 35, 38, 68–69)
Paprika (23, 60, 64)
Parsley (29, 35, 41, 44, 60, 61)
Sage (85)
Thyme (63)
Turmeric (60)

DEEP FREEZE

Asparagus (26)
Baby onions (35, 86)
Broccoli (28, 36, 41, 63)
Cauliflower florets (23, 36)
Green beans (28, 42)
Ice cream (52)
Macaroni cheese (24)
Mixed vegetables (29, 33, 38, 46)
MUSHROOMS
ONIONS
Oven chips (43)
PEAS (23, 25, 45, 47, 58)
PIZZA (36)
Puff pastry* (54)
Ratatouille (20, 21)
Rice (22, 24, 33)
Spinach (25, 28, 48)
Stir fry vegetables (31)
Strawberries (53)
Sweetcorn (23, 24, 29, 48, 58, 70–72)

DAIRY FRIDGE

BUTTER
Cheddar (23, 24, 63)
Cheese (any old) (20, 38, 48, 60, 67–72, 87)
Cottage cheese (28, 29, 58, 61, 62, 63, 70–72, 80)
Edam (30, 41, 46, 67–72)
FRUIT JUICE
　Grapefruit (74)
　Mango (try Indian shop!)
　Orange (75)
　Pineapple (74)
　Tomato (76)
MARGARINE (vegetable)
MILK
Mozzarella (25, 67–72)
Parmesan (27)
Processed cheese (45)
Single cream (22, 25, 36)
Smoked cheese (67–72)
Sour cream (29, 30)

Whipped cream (spray can) (52, 77)
Yoghurt (plain) (62, 64)

FRESH FRUIT 'N' VEG

Apples (53, 54, 59, 62, 76)
Avocado (59, 61)
Bananas (52, 53, 55, 88)
Beansprouts (31, 32, 42, 70–72)
Beetroot (38, 58, 70–72)
BIG BAKING POTATOES (29, 30, 36, 82)
Broccoli (28, 36, 41, 63)
Brussels sprouts (34, 86)
Carrots (31, 59, 60, 62, 63, 79, 85, 87)
Cauliflower florets (24, 36)
Celery (24, 42, 57, 58, 62, 70–72, 87)
Chicory (59)
Chinese leaf (31, 58)
Courgettes (48, 62)
Cress (58, 70–72, 87)
Cucumber (57, 64, 70–72)
Garlic (22, 25, 36, 38, 41, 61)
Lemons (76, 88)
Lettuce (30, 34, 57, 70–72, 82)
Lime (74)
Marrow (44)
Mushrooms (21, 22, 23, 25, 26, 31, 33, 35, 41, 44, 46, 80, 86)
New potatoes (29, 38, 70–72, 79, 81)
ONIONS (24, 28, 31, 33, 38, 41, 42, 44, 45, 47, 60, 61)
Orange (53, 75, 88)
Parsley (29, 35, 41, 44, 60, 61)
Pear (53, 54)
Peppers (28, 57, 58, 59, 70–72)
Red cabbage (38, 58)
Sage (85)
Tomatoes (34, 35, 38, 58, 61, 64, 67–72, 86)
White cabbage (31, 36, 38, 58, 60)

DELICATESSEN COUNTER

Falafel (34)
Fresh pasta
Halva (55)
Hummous (34)
Ready made pie crust (79)

OFF LICENCE

Bitter lemon (74)
Brandy (53)
Cheap red wine (76)
Fizzy mineral water (74)
Galliano (75)
Gin (74)
Grenadine (75)
Sherry (54, 88)
Tequila (75)
Tonic water (73)
Vodka (73, 74, 76)
White rum (74, 75)

HEALTH FOOD STORE

Alfalfa sprouts (59, 70–72)
Apple juice concentrate (74)
'Bacon bits' (45)
'Burgamix' (45, 46, 85)
Christmas pud (veg) (87)
Cinnamon stick (77)
Ginger root (77)
Ginseng root (77)
Meatless steaks (42)
Mince pies (veg) (87)
Miso (70–72)
Sandwich spread (70–72)
Sausalatas (70–72)
'Sizzles' (45)
Sosmix (43, 44, 79, 85)
Soya chunks (48)
Soya mince (47, 48)
Soy sauce, tamari (31, 34, 42, 59, 76)
Tartex (see Sandwich spread)
Tofu (49, 60, 70–72)

INDIAN SHOP

Cardamom pods (77)
Curry paste (33, 47)
Mango juice (74)
Fresh coriander (try in curries)

BOOKSHOP
More copies of "THE JUNK FOOD VEGETARIAN" (!)

16

EPILOGUE

(thanks to Dennis Pedersen for the photo)

THE LAST THING YOU NEED TO KNOW

Jonathan Cainer is twenty-seven years old. He has been a vegetarian all his life.

He leads an unconventional lifestyle, writing books and computer programs. These are mainly on the subject of astrology, which is his burning passion.

At various points in the past Jon has managed a restaurant (in Los Angeles) and a professional recruitment agency (in Leeds).

A lapsed member of a quasi-religious vegetarian spiritual movement, he reneagued on his vows of chastity, celibacy and adzuki beans and escaped to a small North London flat. Here, in a kitchen the size of a broomcupboard, he became a 'Junk Food Vegetarian'.

Jon stresses that: '*The Junk Food Vegetarian* is not just a collection of recipes; it is an alternative lifestyle to the alternative lifestyle. An attitude. A philosophy. A state of being . . .(!)'

He has never been to Oxford, Cambridge, India or San Francisco.